THE RIGHT

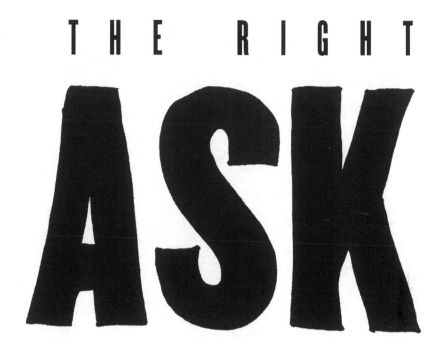

ASK

What Every Advancement
Officer Should Know

by
Michael Y. Warder Sr.

The Right Ask:
What Every Advancement Officer Should Know

For information about reproducing parts of this material:
Contact:
The Warder Consultancy LLC
2172 Malati Circle
Upland, California 91784

Library of Congress

Philanthropy

ISBN-13: 978-1545194454
ISBN-10: 1545194459

Cover and Book Design by Maureen Panos

Printed in the United States of America

For Cheryl, who has been with me all along the way.

TABLE OF CONTENTS

Preface

For more than forty-five years I have worked for all manner of non-profit organizations and have generally been involved with raising resources for them by asking people for help. I also have been the corporate treasurer for multiple organizations. These have included religious organizations, various causes, public events, public policy research organizations or "think tanks," scholarship funds, and colleges. Locations include the East Coast, the Midwest, and the West Coast. I have done door-to-door, direct mail campaigns, and made presentations for gifts greater than $1 million dollars. It has been so much a part of my life that what seems natural to me is a largely an unknown world to others. Along the way, I have helped others to pick up the trade of what is variously called fundraising, development, or advancement. Further, I have entertained many different types of questions and concerns from donors. From time to time, people have suggested that I put something in writing about fundraising. This is it.

In addition to being of practical use for a person starting out in his career as an advancement officer, it might also be of interest to someone who has just been asked to donate to a seemingly important institution that purports to do good things. How do you evaluate the organization? It really is the flip side of the person who is making the request for the donation from that person. Nonetheless, this book is primarily for the person whose task is to raise funds for the cause.

I am not an attorney, a Certified Public Accountant (CPA), or a Certified Financial Planner (CFP), but I have dealt with them throughout my professional life. I urge all readers to seek specific professional counsel should they choose to act on anything mentioned in this book. This effort is more on the order of personal reflections from experience about raising funds generally for non-profits and politics.

Michael Y. Warder, Sr.
Principal
The Warder Consultancy LLC
Upland, California
June 2017

CHAPTER I
What is the Donor Thinking?

"…it is more blessed to give than receive."

WHY GIVE?

THAT BRIEF QUOTE ABOVE is what the Apostle Paul told some early Christians in Greece that Jesus taught.[1] Most of us have heard it since we were children. It seems at first glance to be a paradox. How are we to understand this extraordinary statement? Who doesn't like to receive gifts? After all, it is human nature to enjoy a gift of good food, clothes, jewelry, and such. Think of a birthday party or Christmas morning. We all would like to accumulate enough funds to own a nice home for our family, a car, some discretionary funds, and the security of having adequate resources. And, if we have these things in some amount, we are thankful for having them. Moreover, the paradoxical statement from Paul is not qualified as something unique to early Christians. It is a categorical assertion about giving and receiving that applies to everyone for all time. Nonetheless, if you give something of value away, you don't have it anymore. You have lost it. How can that be a blessing? Why would someone give something of value away?

More recently in the realm of our more familiar pop culture the Beatles have opined, "Money can't buy me love." Nor can it buy friendship, social acceptance, and the respect and esteem of those who matter to us. How do people gain these things? It is by giving something of value that helps another person, a community, or a cause. This book mostly refers to monetary gifts, but perhaps a few examples might make the point. Someone dives into a river to rescue a person from a sinking car. That rescued person has forever enormous gratitude toward that person and so does the family. Those watching on the river bank gratefully acknowledge a sacrificial act made for a stranger. The rescuer could have just watched the car submerge, calculating that they might die in making the effort to rescue a stranger. Or teachers, who on their own volition, give their time to help repeatedly students after class. The pupil never forgets this favorite teacher. Or think of scientists who work their whole lives to develop medicines that help millions of people, most of whom are unborn at the time. They receive the thanks of many, the respect of peers, and institutions are named after them. There is something in human nature that does prompt us to give, and the rewards are not only monetary. Man is, after all, a social being. From the earliest age, we receive from our parents and others and, in time, we do the same for our children and our communities. Some give more than others. And some give to one thing and not another.

Giving often means writing a check for a cause that seeks help. For most people writing a check is easier once they have some degree of financial security. It further helps if their children are successfully educated and launched, and they have some discretionary resources that could be donated to a cause about which they feel strongly. Still, examples abound of those who do not have much by way of personal resources but who, nonetheless, help others.

Some genuinely feel they cannot write a check for a charity or some cause. Many people are struggling to survive and living pay check to pay check. Others would rather accumulate wealth to insure further their financial well-being in case of a sensed looming catastrophe. Others, often exceptionally wealthy, would rather have a bigger house, exotic cars, memberships in the best social clubs, fabulous clothes and jewelry. They devote most of their waking moments to increasing their net worth to show their peers that they are somehow better. Despite these acquisitions, it is well known that a high net worth does not guarantee happiness.

Still others, usually the super wealthy, create and invest their lives in developing goods or services that benefit millions. They are driven. Yes, they are wealthy, but it is not the accumulation of wealth that drives them. It is a by-product. Andrew Carnegie, John D. Rockefeller, and Henry Ford are examples of people who grew vast fortunes through hard work and brilliant minds in service to mastering, respectively, the steel, oil, and auto industries. Millions of people benefitted. More recently Bill Gates has accumulated an extraordinary fortune through the development and sale of operating systems for computers and related software. Warren Buffett has been uniquely successful in investing in companies and making millions of dollars for his shareholders and for the companies in which he invested. These people eventually did plow their wealth into charities that benefitted many people whether in public libraries, education, or scientific and medical research. Mr. Gates and Mr. Buffett have tried in recent years to spread the idea among the super wealthy to take a pledge to give away more than half of the wealth they have accumulated, either while they are alive or at death. After all, with a net worth of over $86 billion, Mr. Gates, [2] can only use so much of it for personal enjoyment. Still, some people believe that using their accumulated capital to develop even more wealth is the way to go.

Carlos Slim of Mexico, one of the wealthiest men in the world, with a net worth of around $55 billion,[3] was asked a few years back in a room full of wealthy business owners and CEO's at a Forbes conference, why he didn't take the pledge that many of the super wealthy have taken to give away more than half of their wealth. His answer at that time was that he thought by using his capital wisely, he could continue to invest it in businesses that would provide more people with employment opportunities. These jobs would lift millions of people out of poverty. Well, who can argue that Mr. Slim is morally wrong? Still, he will not live forever. What will become of his wealth after his death when he can no longer direct his capital in such a productive way? As the adage goes, "you can't take it with you." Nor can you direct it from beyond the grave. You are dead.

Some would argue that the solution to the Slim situation, is for government to take an ample percentage of the wealth. They believe the estate tax, or as some call it the "death tax," might solve the "problem." Interestingly, Mexico does not have an estate tax. Mr. Slim is safe in that regard. On the other hand, Japan has an estate tax that goes up to 55%.[4] In the United States, as of this writing in 2017, the estate tax is 40% for any dollar over $5.49 million for a single person's estate.[5] There is intense discussion on this tax. There always is. It is an easily demonstrable proposition that government would not use this capital more efficiently of all the options one might consider whether they be family, designated heirs, charities, or even the companies from which the wealth derived. Government is not known to be either efficient or effective in terms of achieving its objectives.

There are many people who believe they are sufficiently well-off so they might consider helping others beyond their own family. For all the effort and intelligence people invest in accumulating wealth, they should use a similar effort in deploying it in any act of charity. Too often persons of wealth do not put much thought or analysis into what they support. A good advancement officer should be able to advise the donor as to why a gift to a particular organization is the right decision for that donor. The premise of the book is that giving and receiving are two sides of the same coin.

THE SPECIFIC CAUSE

Let's assume potential donors, often called prospects, have accumulated enough, or at least are generating enough money, that they could give something to help their fellow man. Further, they would like to give. Why should donors give their money, time or expertise to help a specific organization? The short answer is donors must understand and believe in the stated purpose. They must believe that an organization is unique in its ability to accomplish that purpose. This may sound simple. It is not. Put in this way, it is, after all, an abstract organization that could stand for anything.

Whether wealthy or not, all of us are bombarded daily through mail, television, radio, social media, and friends to give money, time and attention to a myriad of worthy causes. And there are hundreds of thousands of organizations that compete for people to give, whether it be churches, schools, colleges, hospitals and medical research institutions, theater groups, museums, welfare organizations, advocacy groups, think tanks, candidates for political office, etc. Each of them have their own special kind of appeal. A church is quite different than a university. A hospital is quite different than a candidate running for office. Somehow advancement officers, sometimes called solicitors or fundraisers, must break through this cacophony of supplications to make the case as to why their cause is superior to the others. If not superior, the cause needs to be seen by the donor as at least worthy of some support.

PERSONAL CONNECTION

Usually there is some personal connection to a cause that prompts a person to consider a request for a gift. Perhaps a family is deeply appreciative of the care a loved one received while in a specific hospital. Maybe the spiritual sustenance and moral guidance through sermons, fellowship, and summer camps that a family receives from a local church prompts a gift. A graduate of a college may feel gratitude toward their alma mater for the education received, friendships made, and the subsequent benefits they acquired. Public policy research organizations (think tanks) and advocacy groups may appeal to prospects who believe in the principles, ideas, and activities of a group that advances a cause that they read about in the newspaper or, increasingly, on line. Maybe a family that was flooded out of their home and received aid in a time of desperate need decides later to make a gift to the group. Perhaps a young person received attention at a local club for youth that helped them on their path to a rewarding life. Often a gift to an institution is prompted by being touched by it in a personal way.

Another way people are prompted to give to an organization is that friends are involved in a non-profit organization. Friends invite friends to a dinner, a golf tournament, a speech, a conference, or a performance as an introduction to what this organization or cause is about. They encourage their friends to get involved. It is another kind of personal connection. A good advancement officer should be alert as to whom is touched by their organization.

FEDERAL ENCOURAGEMENT THROUGH TAX LAW

In addition to some personal connection to a specific organization, in the United States the federal government and the fifty states all encourage charitable gifts through offering tax incentives. The idea is that private and often local charitable initiatives should be encouraged to advance the general well-being of our society. Some activities are judged to be worthy of such encouragement. If donors give to charities, they may deduct that amount from their taxable income. I should quickly add that a donor needs to seek specific advice from tax counsel as the laws and regulations regarding charitable gifts can be complex. A gift need not be simply writing a check in a certain year. These different types of gifts and some strategic considerations will be discussed in more detail in Chapter V.

It is true that the government of the United States passes laws that require us to "give" money each year to the government to support the common good. These are not gifts freely given. Citizens are compelled to pay taxes under penalty of laws passed by our elected officials and enforced by the executive branch of government. On behalf of the government, employers withhold federal and state taxes from our paychecks. Still, tax dollars do support the common good. Then, why would the government encourage private charity on top of these taxes? In fact, many governments of other countries do not encourage charity in the same way. Indeed, some governments feel threatened by large charities operating without the direct control of the government.

The United States is a large country with over 320 million citizens. In our history, there has been a tradition and ethos of pitching in at the local level to help one another. People through voluntary local associations would build churches, schools, barns, and hospitals and all manner of things. British philosopher Edmund Burke called these voluntary associations the "little platoons" that stood between the individual and the state. Through them people at the local level solved many problems. By the time federal tax dollars are redistributed locally, they go through many levels of approvals that take time and money. In the end, they may not be timely or on target for local needs. This is especially so for the federal government. Increasingly it is also the case in large state governments. Private charity frequently is more effective and efficient. It is often direct help given at the location of the problem by people who can see the results. Thus, it is encouraged by our tax laws. A person who raises money for a non-profit charitable organization needs a working familiarity with the possible tax benefits of a charitable gift.

Citizens living in countries where there is no tax-incentive to encourage charity will do so for the same reasons as any American. It is just that there is no tax incentive. Charity, like compassion, is not unique to America.

LAWS, REGULATIONS, AND THE COURTS

In the United States, after the federal tax laws come the regulations of the Internal Revenue Service, more commonly called the IRS. If you are on an airplane and don't wish to talk to the chatty person next to you, tell them you are thinking of a career working for the IRS. It is not a beloved agency. Nonetheless, the government, with the approval of the Congress and the President, collects taxes on our behalf for the general welfare of the country. It is worth restating that it is "we the people" who pay for every penny. It falls to the IRS to translate these tax laws into regulations. Since they keep increasing each year, experts sometimes argue about how many pages are in the IRS code. At the end of 2016 there were about 98,000 pages.[6] The average bible is about 1,200 pages, but at least no one has added to the Christian bible since about the 4th century AD. The United States Congress adds each year to our tax laws, while the IRS dutifully follows with appropriate regulations. That is complicated enough, but there is a further wrinkle. When there is a dispute about the precise application of the law and the regulations in a case, the matter goes to court, and a decision is made there. So, court decisions also guide citizens and charities about philanthropy. For most people, they simply fill out the 1040A or the 1040EZ. Most will just take standard deductions and be happy. Many others do not do this, as they have a small business, a home, capital gains or losses, real estate taxes, and various kinds of assets that effect state filings that in turn effect federal filings.

As I said at the outset, I am not a tax attorney. Advancement officers should not try to pretend to be one. If advancement officers are advising donors about how to fill out tax forms, they have stepped over the line. Having said that, the basic idea of US tax code is that if a person has an income of $100,000, and they make a gift to a charity of $1,000, they can be taxed on $99,000. For people of wealth that have mortgages, stocks, a business or businesses, children, grandchildren, etc., other complications set in. While there are some tax basics about which advancement officers should know, they should also know their limits.

A Word about the Flat Tax

I will discuss taxes in greater depth in Chapter III, but I should add a word here about one special tax idea. Every four years aspiring Presidential nominees run on something called the flat tax. They say it would be so easy that a person could fill out their taxes on a post card. It goes something like this. Every person and every business would be taxed 17% on their income. Or maybe 19%. There would be no distinction between regular salary, dividends and interest payments, corporate business income, and capital gains tax. All these taxes would be 17%, or some such number. Billionaires and their secretaries would be taxed at the same rates. No special considerations for a whole range of deductions for the wealthy. The flat tax really has an appeal.

As of 2017 there are seven levels of taxation with those earning little paying 10% and the wealthiest (for a married couple) paying 39.6% on each dollar earned above $466,950.[7] There likely will be changes in these tax rates in the future. There always are. In this year of 2017, the discussions seem more serious. Older persons of wealth, or tax historians, will recall in the 1950s that the highest tax rate was 92%. That is right. 92%. Therefore, the very wealthy hired lawyers and accountants to find ways around paying the full freight through loopholes in the tax code. The effective rate, after all the legal exemptions, was much less. The same is true today. Wealthy people hire attorneys and accountants to reduce the effective rate they pay. Associations and lobbyists make a good living in Washington, DC and in state capitols persuading elected officials for exceptions.

Usually the candidate advocating the flat tax will say that deductions for charitable gifts and interest paid on home mortgages would be allowed. So, right at the outset, even they make exceptions. They say that because there otherwise would be no chance to be nominated by either of the major political parties. The charities and the real estate industry throughout America would mobilize. But, given a crisis, you never know. In the 1970s, interest paid on credit cards was a deduction. That is hard to believe these days. At the time, there was a war on inflation and an effort to dampen consumer spending. There is also the ever-present need for government to raise revenue to pay for government spending. The deduction of credit card interest was eliminated. No Presidential candidate has yet been elected on the flat tax since the federal income tax law of 1913. It appeals to the majority that the seriously wealthy should pay a higher percentage than the rate the average person pays. As of this writing the top 1% of wage earners pay about 38% of the total federal income tax.[8]

The couple that has an income above $466,950 knows that for each dollar of charity that they give above that magic number, they reduce their tax liability by almost 40%. While the tax incentives decrease for people with lesser incomes, the same principle applies at each level of the federal income tax code. Advancement officers need to be sensitive to these realities.

TELEVISION TESTIMONIALS

Many charities use testimonials to elicit gifts. There is no question that these are important. The television ad shows the young child happily making progress to overcome a physical challenge. Another might show a veteran coming back to a more normal life through therapy after losing his legs in battle so that we might keep our freedom. There are the puppies at the local animal shelter who stare at the camera with soulful eyes while "Silent Night" plays in the background. If we are human, it is hard not to respond to these appeals. Perhaps there is a video of a family getting back on their feet after an earthquake, flood, or wildfire who is grateful for emergency support. A public policy research organization, a think tank, might have a respected government official say how valuable the research is and how it helped him in making decisions.

These appeals, created by people who know how to elicit human response from the most cold-hearted person, may move a person to give $19.99 a month by calling a telephone number, and giving the credit card info over the phone. All who respond to these pitches should dig a little deeper into the nature and performance of any charity to insure it is the best use of their own limited resources. These testimonials are also made in direct mail solicitations and, increasingly, emails, Facebook, Twitter, and other social media. The advancement officer who works for these organizations should be prepared to answer questions about the cost of these ads, and how much of the donation goes to the primary mission. Serious donors will want answers to these questions. In many instances these appeals do more for the agency that creates and places the ads than for the charity. This approach needs scrutiny before being launched and while in operation. The money raised may not justify the expense. Serious advancement officers would be wise to know these financial details.

LEADERSHIP

Before they open that checkbook or click the "donate" prompt on that website, people should first look to see if they trust the leader of any institution. Leaders come in all shapes and sizes. Some are charismatic with a gift of persuasion. Others seem to radiate a seriousness of intent, a knowledge of the organization, and the purpose it serves. Some talk a lot. Some don't. Some are show horses; some are work horses. Some see the big picture; others master the details. One constant that is required above all else is integrity. If the person leading the organization gives indication of something less than integrity, it is time for the advancement officer to start looking for employment elsewhere.

The donor needs to know about who is managing the gift they give. If advancement officers do not know much about the President, or Chief Executive Officer (CEO), they are in a weak position to ask for a gift. Rightly so. How long has the leader been at the institution? Does the leader have a reputation for integrity and competence? Is there evidence of a deep commitment to the mission of the organization? What have they accomplished in the past? What credentials do they have? Why did they leave one organization to move to another? Do they seem knowledgeable about the organization they lead? If the solicitor cannot testify to the character and ability of the CEO, it is difficult to ask for a gift from a potential donor.

The leader of an institution that depends on donations needs to be available to donors. Presentations, award dinners, conferences, briefings, and one-on-one appointments are some of the ways. Nonetheless, no one who runs a large organization can spend all their time meeting donors. They should be leading the program officers to make sure they are effectively accomplishing the goals of the organization.

They also need to make sure that funds are managed and invested wisely and that the organization is not wasteful. No one wants to give to an organization that is providing the good life for its leaders and employees but not achieving its greater goals. In any case, the CEO does need to spend time meeting with his supporters, calling them on the phone, or writing them personal letters. Television and radio interviews can help as do articles in local newspapers or references in the social media.

It is true that some organizations are so well known and enjoy such a good public reputation, that the specific leader may not be as important. Many people would say the Salvation Army has a reputation for integrity. Still, if anyone is considering a gift, it is good to know about the CEO. If it is a national charity, it is good to know who is running the local operation. I do recall that several years ago, a major well known national charity had a scandal derived from the fact that the long-time CEO approved contracts for services to companies in which had a financial interest. It was a crisis that caused a major reformation from top to bottom. We are dealing with human institutions after all. Integrity and competence at the top is vital. Leaders are human beings with the same foibles we all have. Those who ask for gifts from prospects, need to be able to testify to the integrity and competence of the leadership.

A brief story will illustrate the importance of the leader. On July 8, 2016, a man died in Pakistan. His name was Abdul Sattar Edhi.[9] His death was marked all around the world. He could raise enough money in Pakistan to have 1,800 ambulance vans, 28 rescue boats, 2 jets, and a helicopter. He also had a variety of medical centers. He received the resources needed to acquire these since he started his Edhi Foundation in 1951. He rescued people in need. It was his ambulance that received the call to pick up slain *Wall Street Journal* journalist Daniel Pearl in 2002. Mr. Edhi's wife, Bilquis, continues to oversee the maternity and adoption services of the Edhi Foundation. When Edhi died, the Prime Minister of Pakistan declared a national day of mourning and honored him with a state funeral. Pakistan's army chief and others attended his funeral in the National Stadium, and the army fired a 19 gun salute out of respect. He lived in a windowless room in a Karachi slum and owned 2 sets of clothes. He insisted that he be buried in one of them.

I asked one prominent Pakistani who lives now in America if he knew about him. He said Edhi is revered by all regardless of religion and that he was a living saint. He said he was the richest man in all of Pakistan. I inquired about him to a young Pakistani selling tee-shirts at a mall here in Southern California. He said with great affection that one day Edhi was standing in the road, and as the cars went by people just gave him cash, jewels, and gold such was their trust in him. It was all in a pile. This young person's father gave to him on that occasion and could touch him. It was one of the highlights of this man's life. Few could do what this great man has done in a country that is not wealthy by most standard measures. Nonetheless, his life makes the point. Giving is a powerful and blessed thing. The person at the top is key. They need not be saints. They should have a deserved reputation for honesty and competence.

LEADERSHIP OLD AND NEW

Evaluating leaders can provide a great insight into any organization. Many non-profits are first started by a founder who has a vision, passion and charisma. Without these, few organizations can get started. It is also true, that more than a few non-profits with great missions are harmed if the founder, or the CEO, stays on too long. It happens. Sometimes there develops in these situations a feeling that the CEO is indispensable. The Board of such an organization often lacks the will to make the hard decision to thank the CEO for his service and to let him know it is time for a change. This is a critical moment in the life of any non-profit. Nonetheless, the wheel turns. As someone once said, "cemeteries are filled with indispensable leaders."

How does an organization know when it's time for a new CEO? Physical age can be a general indicator. It is true that one person may be an old 75 and another may be a young 80. But most people at that age tend to rely on the tried and true of the past. They often, though not always, become risk averse. If the same person has led an organization for more than 20 or 25 years, doubtless the question arises if the purpose is to employ the CEO or to accomplish the mission. The mission and strategic plan to achieve it are the North star and compass of the organization.

Regardless of age and length of service, there are questions that need to be kept in mind. Are opportunities being missed? Has revenue slumped? What do the other indicators, or measures, of success show? Is the organization using the force multipliers of new technology? Have the auditors noticed some problems? Is the annual dinner losing steam? Does overall impact seem stagnant or diminished? Chances are if an advancement officer is asking these questions, so are the potential donors. Significant donors did not get where they are in life by being unobservant.

Boards need to be sensitive to know when it is time to change the leadership. It is their most important function. Usually, and especially if it is the founding CEO, there needs to be a strategic planning process for a decision to be made about the future vision of the organization. This can be awkward since it is usually the CEO who has recruited the board members. Advocating a change in leadership in such a circumstance could be taken as disloyalty to the CEO. Nonetheless, the most important object of loyalty should be loyalty to the mission of the organization.

What will the organization look like when the founding CEO, or the long-time CEO, is gone? What now are the needed attributes of a new leader in the life of the organization? I was the Chief Development Officer (CDO) for a non-profit and recall a retreat for senior management and a few board members where the planning facilitator asked the founding CEO to take a chair and put it outside the group chair arrangement. The facilitator forbade him to talk while the rest spoke about the future vision for the organization. You could have cut the atmosphere with a knife. We then discussed and listed the standard SWOT analysis: Strengths. Weaknesses. Opportunities. Threats. The facilitator was highly skilled, sensitive, and decisive. Sometimes it takes an outsider to step in to facilitate seeing the organization beyond the current leader. The person who normally organized and led these annual retreats had recruited this special facilitator, and this time was in a support role for the meeting. The founding CEO realized that it was the right thing to do, and all things considered, took it very well. I continue to have great admiration for this person. The organization took on a second life as it passed through this crucial time, with the support of the founding CEO.

BOARD OF DIRECTORS

Another way a potential donor may evaluate an organization is to look at the Board of Directors, or Trustees. These people have fiduciary responsibility for the integrity of the organization. Who are they? Do they enjoy a reputation for integrity and accomplishment? Do they themselves support the organization either through gifts of money, time, or expertise? Do they meet quarterly? Does the organization have a variety of types of people representing different sectors of the community?

In most non-profit organizations, the Board will meet quarterly and provide valuable oversight. As mentioned, it is they who are responsible to hire and, if need be, fire the chief executive. They also approve the budget that the CEO presents to them. Or they do not. They will approve, or not, the financial package for the compensation of the CEO. Of course, every meeting of the board does not deal with hiring or firing the CEO or approving the budget. Nonetheless, they usually will be evaluating how the organization is doing in terms of where it is in relation to the mission, the strategic plan, the goals and the allotted budget. Frequently, in larger non-profits they will break up into committees that will evaluate more deeply the programs, fundraising, internal controls (spending and approvals), money management, and investment results. They, or a committee of the Board, generally have a say on which company will be hired to provide the annual audited financial statement. Usually Boards have a defined term of three or four years. The specifics of the term are determined by the by-laws which are filed, along with the articles of incorporation, with the state in which they operate. These documents are filed initially when the organization is founded. They can be amended if, in the opinion of the Board, they need to be. These, along with the accounting records, can be made available so a prospect can satisfy their own sense of due diligence. Rarely does a prospect ask to see these documents.

As a rule, it is a healthy sign if board members do not stay on decade after decade. These types of long serving board members do not bring fresh eyes to evaluate performance. Maybe they have grown used to problems the organization has and just accepts them. Personal friendships with the CEO may cause them to excuse poor performance. It is frequently the case that board members do stay on too long and bring nothing new to the deliberations. Instead of suggesting corrective actions before a crisis, they may allow the organization to drift.

In addition to financial support, board members should have a diversity of professional experience. Ideally, any non-profit would be well-served to have an attorney, a certified public accountant, a public relations executive, a non-profit professional, and an investment professional on the Board. Each can bring a perspective that can sharpen the overall performance of the organization.

Best practices advise that the President not be a member of the Board of Directors. The reason for that is simple enough. The Board may feel they cannot cross swords with a peer on the Board. If the CEO votes on a budget, it includes his compensation. Some organizations allow the CEO to be a board member, and in some cases it may work. It gives me caution if the CEO is a board member. It is a large red flag if a board member also receives compensation from the organization. If several members of the Board receive compensation, it makes it difficult for an advancement officer to ask prospects for support. Board members who are officers or key program directors, and who receive salaries, have a conflict of interest. They also may detract from the key role the Board of Directors are supposed to play.

Since the Board has fiduciary responsibility for the organization to make sure the donations are directed for the purposes of the organization, they can be held legally liable for any violations of law. A government agency or an aggrieved party, like a disgruntled employee or a donor, might hold the board member liable for alleged misbehavior. They might be subject to lawsuits for monetary damages. Often organizations will buy Directors and Officers Liability Insurance to mitigate such risk.

Perhaps most essentially, the board members should have an ability to give annual donations or multi-year gifts. Board members who donate have "skin in the game." By doing so, they indicate that they believe in the organization. An educational organization that has a board with a majority of professors is asking for trouble. Why? The concern has nothing to do with each person. It concerns the fact that they collectively offer too narrow a focus for the many functions of a non-profit, tax-exempt organization. Further, academics may not have the capacity to support financially the charity. If the Board, with a broad range of occupations and experience, supports the organization with gifts, it indicates they believe in the organization. It shows strength and health.

It is difficult for a solicitor to ask a potential donor to give to a public charity if the officers and board members are composed of family members. I know of a non-profit tax-exempt organization where the husband and wife hold corporate offices and one of the children is the office manager. The potential for self-dealing and management sloppiness is too tempting. Even if all involved were saints, it is just not sound practice as even saints fall short of perfection. Why tempt them?

There is a caveat about family members and possible self-dealing that involves a particular kind of tax-exempt charitable organization. Say a family is led by a husband and wife and they have made a large amount of money over their life. They discuss with their accountant and attorney a plan to set up a grant-giving family foundation and put, say, ten million dollars into it to help charities. It is their money. They and their children may be on the Board. Each year the family foundation makes donations to worthy charitable organizations. This is quite common and more than acceptable. The parents are "giving back" and they are teaching their children to do the same through this grant giving. This type of charitable foundation gives money to other charities. They do not receive donations from the public. However, these founding donors should not be receiving a salary. If they or their children do receive a salary, they may be in violation of tax laws. Regardless, such an arrangement raises red flags.

These days, communities are large and spread out, and it is difficult to know the inner workings of any group. It is also difficult for a solicitor of an organization who is not involved directly with the inner dynamics of the Board of Directors and the CEO to testify about these matters to donors. Nonetheless, people want to be assured that the group does what it represents it does. What tools are available to advancement officers to answer some of these questions and concerns that a donor may have? They are, after all, the people who go out and ask for donations.

OUTSIDE AUDITOR

The annual audit, conducted by an outside firm, is to state if the financial records of the company are fairly and accurately represented. The product is the annual audited financial statement. It is another check to see if the organization is legitimate. The key person doing the audit should be a Certified Public Accountant, or CPA. This credential assures the public that the examining company is authoritative in such examinations.

Who checks to make sure the auditors are legitimate? Such certification comes from the American Institute of Certified Public Accountants.[10] This organization, established in 1887, has over 400,000 members in 144 countries. They have various specialties of certification, one of which is for non-profit organizations.

Even here there are some cautions. If the outside auditor has been evaluating the books of an organization for many, many years, it may indicate a problem. Why? Well there is a conflict of interest in that the non-profit organization pays the firm for the audit. If they do it year after year, the audit company may pull some punches to keep the revenue stream going. It is important to remember that while the non-profit, or the profit-making company for that matter, pays the auditor, the auditor does its work on behalf of the public. That is why a proper auditor is called a Certified PUBLIC Accountant. In the end, their good reputation is all they have. If they make a public statement that the financial records represent fairly the financial records and activities and they do not do so, the auditor and the organization both have a serious problem. It is good to have a new auditor every so often. It is inconvenient because the organization must explain the operations to a new auditor, but in so doing they may discover better ways to operate. It is healthy. Also, by putting the audit business out to bid, the organization may get a less expensive audit that is just as authoritative.

The audit of an organization by a well-recognized regional, or even national, CPA firm gives more credibility. A local one-person shop run by a CPA may do a great job at a bargain price, but again there is the question of being captured by the organization. Is this CPA needy for the business? Would the firm overlook some problems to keep the business? It is hard to know. A larger well established firm would rather lose the account than bend their standards, and lose their reputation for integrity. Well, these too are human beings, and few saints if any, historically, are CPAs. (In case you are interested to know, the patron saint of auditors is St. Matthew. According to the Gospels, he was a tax collector from Capernaum. Not quite the same as an auditor, but close enough.)

Another caution is that the auditor is only allowed to look at the books and related materials. They can examine accounts receivable and the payables. They can look at the investment performance. They can check to see if approvals to spend money have proper internal controls, and that if checks require two signatures, there are, in fact, two signatories every time. They can note internal inconsistencies and attempt to resolve them. Fixed assets are checked to make sure nothing is missing. They can ask to see most anything, but they can only evaluate matters based on what they are given. If a treasurer or other key corporate officer presents them with false documentation that seems legitimate, they cannot be held liable. And they state that in every audit.

Usually the auditors present a draft audit to the CEO, the Chief Financial Officer (CFO), and the Treasurer. Sometimes the non-profit's legal counsel is present. I have served as Treasurer in the past and found these sessions quite productive. Some Boards may have an audit committee whose job is to review the draft audit. Internal controls might be improved to ensure that expenditures are properly reviewed before the check is written. Or perhaps the organization has bills for the past fiscal year that came in late because there was a failure to notify vendors. So, the payables may not be accurate. There should be consistency on these policies and performance from year to year to reflect the year over year realities of the organization. Another question might arrive if a donor is late in his annual payment for a $3,000,000 multi-year gift. Such pledges must be accounted for in the balance sheet. They derive from a pledge agreement that the donor and the President of the non-profit sign. It is a contract. Year one may have been fine, but what if the donor cannot make future payments due to financial hardship? These changing developments must be reflected in the books. A footnote needs to be added with a change to the balance sheet. The matter needs to be disclosed to the Board. These things happen to every non-profit, and they need to be disclosed in the audited financial statement.

Some might think that such a pledge agreement should not be on the books to begin with. After all, the organization has not received it. Yet failure to disclose such a gift agreement, or contract, might give a false impression as to the strength of the organization. An unethical leader might say there is desperate need, when there is not, because of such a significant multi-year commitment.

In addition, footnotes might need to be reviewed about a material change in the organization after the end of the accounting period. Suppose on December 31, the end of the accounting year for an organization, everything looks good. But, in the next month the organization encounters a catastrophe in January. The audit comes out in March. The material change in the status of the organization needs to be noted, even though it occurs after the end of the fiscal year but before the publication of the audit.

In mentioning these matters, I do not wish to create the impression that non-profits are usually not worthy of trust. Most do good works vital to the community, the nation, and even the world. Most auditors do a trustworthy professional audit. But just as when an investor seeks to invest in a company, there are rules about what should be disclosed. There are good reasons for these rules. Too often, a thoughtful investor, who does due diligence before investing hard-earned money or someone else's, throws off their analytical skills when making a gift to a charity. It is wise to be a prudent donor as well as a prudent investor.

Usually, people in the advancement department have little idea about the audit, the footnotes, and any changes after the books are closed. To the extent advancement officers are ignorant of these matters, to that same extent they are less authoritative when they ask a potential donor for a large gift. The larger the organization, the more difficult it is for advancement officers to be authoritative. It is the job of the President (CEO) or the Vice President for Advancement (Chief Development Officer, or CDO) to give sufficient information to solicitors so they can effectively do their jobs. There are reasons why non-profits have an annual audit by a certified public accountant. It is to assure the public that the organization is sound. Advancement officers need that same assurance when they ask for support. It is good to know about these matters, especially if asking a prospect for a major gift.

THE 990 FORM

As a matter of practicality, the 990 form is a very good tool to evaluate a non-profit organization that is a charity. It generally is more available than the latest audited financial statement. As a matter of legal requirement, each non-profit charity, except for churches, files a yearly 990 form with the federal government. In this form the organization tells the federal government its revenue and expenses. It reports who is on the Board. It reports the salaries of the corporate officers and the most highly compensated employees. It discloses any compensation for board members. These salary disclosures also include benefits. A donor, or any member of the public with proper notice, has the right to see this document.

This form also breaks out the use of the money received into three categories: Program, Administration, and Development (fundraising). These are important because donors want to know how the organizations uses the gifts they are given. If the organization spends most of its money on fundraising and administration, it raises serious questions about how committed they are to the stated mission. Organizations differ, but it is generally accepted that if 80% is spent on program and the other 20% is spent on administration and advancement, it is good. If an organization spends all it has raising money, it really is self-serving. The auditors look at these ratios with great care noting the methodology for the break outs.

Sometimes the breakouts of Program, Administration, and Fundraising are not what you might expect. I once worked for a non-profit tax-exempt educational and charitable organization that had a direct mail program. Each letter cost one dollar to mail including list rental, postage, printing, envelope stuffing, etc. You might think that the whole expense for that letter would be for fundraising. Not so. The organization had a former IRS senior agent with a law degree as counsel. This highly qualified person read every letter to make sure it was consistent with our educational purpose. We received judgments on category breakouts. If the letter had six sides (3 sheets of paper with content on each side), the attorney would say that five of the six sides were "program" and only one side was "fundraising." The reason was the first five sides were educational since they concerned an issue or the nature of the organization. The request for funds only came in a few sentences on the sixth side. It generally worked out that the direct mail program, when added all up, was 50% program (public information) and 50% fundraising. The auditors were fine with this.

How about that big end of the year dinner where the non-profit has an important guest speaker, awards, and the press in attendance? Annual reports and literature are placed on each seat. The charity requests that each attendee pays $200 for each reservation (the dinner costs $100), $10,000 for special tables, etc. The Chairman of the dinner gives $25,000 for the honor. The President speaks on this occasion to thank everyone and tell them how the year went. They all know it's the annual fundraising dinner. Still, there is an educational component to the event. Call in the auditor for what is a reasonable breakout as to what part is educational and what part is fundraising.

Generally public relations is considered program since it involves educating the public. How about the salary for the President? Salaries and benefits as well as expenses may reasonably be broken out into the three categories, and that is generally by how much time the President devotes to each. The larger the organization, the tighter the categories. The Director of Administration, for example, has his salary and benefits counted 100% toward Administration.

There are some caveats to the general 80%-20% rule. Suppose the charity is trying to raise money to help people with leprosy. This disease is so horrible that people may be afraid to associate with it. It may be much harder to raise the money for leprosy and more resources need to be spent to raise the money.

There are other questions. Television ads ask for support for a worthy cause. It could be for children, disabled veterans, animals that need shelter and the like. Millions of dollars might be raised, but millions of dollars must be spent to raise the money that does help the intended recipients. Suppose one organization raises $1 million and only spends $200,000 for administration and fundraising. Another organization spends $25 million on television ads and raises $50 million for the cause. It is a comparatively bad ratio (Check with the CPA about how much of the ad is "program" and how much is "fundraising.'), but the television ad raises many dollars to go for the intended cause. In those cases, it really is good to look at the 990s. There is the further question of who is receiving that $25 million spent on creating the ads and their placement.

If it is the type of charity that is a grant giving foundation, their 990 also discloses recipient organizations and the amounts it gives to each. In this way, the 990 is also a valuable resource for advancement officers as they can see what types of organizations the foundation funds.

As a matter of practicality, an organization called Guidestar publishes on the Internet these 990 documents for most American charities. There are other sites, but that is the one that I found to be most useful. If an organization does not file a 990, it is a red flag. Charity Navigator, Charity Watch, Give Well are other organizations that evaluate the effectiveness and efficiency of any charity that enjoys a tax-exempt status.

These 990 forms that are published on the Internet at these special websites are generally about two years out of date. The audited financial statement, often less available, should be produced and finalized about three to four months at the close of the fiscal year. The two documents should agree, but they do have different purposes.

Both the audit and the 990 are to assure the donor about the good faith of the charity. There is public accountability. Without these documents, the non-profit is little different than the person at the stoplight who asks for a handout. Should a person give? Of course, it is up to the possible potential donor. There will be no tax deduction and no public accountability for that street corner gift. When a donor gives to a charity to help that same type of person, that charity must be responsible to identify the person who receives the help, whether it be a cot or a warm meal. It might be the gift goes to pay for some classes about how to get a job or how to develop a skill. Presumably the program officers for the non-profit are trained to make sure that the charitable dollars go where they will do the greatest good. That person on the street corner is apt to go buy some alcohol or drugs to get through another day. And the gift would reward that person for standing on that corner and asking for money with no accountability. I knew a minister who always gave something to that guy on the corner. I know others who would say it is wrong. Caveat Donator. Let the donor beware. That advice is true when considering the guy on the street or the non-profit that makes it possible for a gift to be a charitable deduction.

By examining the Board of Directors, the President, the annual audited financial statement, and the most recent 990 form, potential donors can reasonably satisfy themselves that the organization is, or is not, a good place to give. Advancement officers should know this information so they can make the best possible case to the prospect and answer any questions. Not knowing this information may indicate to the potential donor that the solicitor is unpersuasive when compared to other charities who also are seeking support.

Salaries of the Leaders

When looking at the 990 form, a potential donor often wants to know what the leader and key officers receive by way of compensation. Would a prospect give to a charity where the President receives a $500,000 a year compensation package? Or, would a prospect rather give to an organization where the President receives $75,000 a year? The answer is not clear. To put it in the most extreme form, suppose the President with the very large salary runs an organization that has an annual budget of $400 million dollars a year, while the CEO with the $75,000 salary has an annual budget of $100,000 a year? Which leader gives the potential donor more confidence that they are competent at what they do?

There are many non-profits where a CEO receives a salary that is

dren to inherit their faith tradition while they are learning math and reading. To accomplish these ends they pay tuition so their child can attend a private school, even as they pay taxes for the public schools that their children will not attend.

For nearly four years (2001-05) I witnessed this strong parental need to pass on religious teachings to children while working for the Children's Scholarship Fund. I helped raise and administer funds for low-income inner city families for partial tuition scholarships so their children could attend a private school, most of which were religiously affiliated. Many of the wealthy donors would match dollar-for-dollar what two other wealthy donors put up. John Walton, the son of Sam Walton of Walmart, and Ted Forstmann of the New York firm Forstmann & Little, put up $100 million in 1999 to start the national program. My job was to find local partners who would match dollar-for-dollar that $100 million. Both felt that our public education system was failing the upcoming generations. They felt education was key to the future of America, a country that allowed them to prosper. They conceived of the program themselves, and they made a most generous contribution.

For children to qualify for these partial scholarships, I had to examine the most recent IRS income tax filing of the parents, or their monthly welfare statement ("notice of action") issued by the county, before they would get a partial scholarship. Frankly it was staggering to see a family with $24,000 in income put up $1,500 of their own money to send their children to K-8 school whose tuition might be $3,000 a year. At the time that was the average for our office. We would match that money from the parents with ours from the two national donors and from the local donors. We had many more applicants than scholarships, and we awarded the scholarships initially based on a lottery system. Once a family was in the program, we continued to support them until graduation, if the student did the necessary minimum. If the parents were not satisfied with their child's performance, they had "skin in the game" and could pull their child from school. That rarely happened. Families did move out of the school district, and that would result in discontinuance.

In addition to the local churches, synagogues or mosques, often the larger church organization of their denomination would assist with some financial aid. It was also interesting to see that a family of another denomination would send their child to a Catholic school rather than a public school. The difference between the denominations was small when compared with the public schools, and they believed the quality of instruction was superior when compared to some very bad inner city public schools. The teachers and the principals of these schools made less than their public-school counterparts, but it was a calling for them. They also had much less bureaucratic interference from the vast labyrinth of public school administrators and programs.

The model of dollar-for-dollar matching is a powerful technique for raising funds, but it is also valuable in terms of accountability. For every dollar put up by Walton and Forstmann through the New York headquarters, there was a local donor who would put up a dollar. Those two dollars were then matched, on average, by two dollars from the parents. Not only did that initial $100 million grow to $400 million, but there was local engagement and accountability by local philanthropists as well as parental oversight. These thoughtful and generous men are now deceased and the CSF advancement model has changed. Nonetheless, what they started flourishes and remains a tremendous example of generous and focused philanthropy.

A challenge to match dollar-for-dollar is a powerful way to encourage others to give. It is a useful tool for any charity.

Wealthy families will often send their children to much more expensive private schools. Tuition at some of these, especially at the high school level, will often be on a par with college expenses. Even here, there will be a need for donations above and beyond the tuition expense. These schools will have advancement officers who will ask for additional support. It might be for teacher recruitment, science equipment, a football stadium, computers and software for the administra-

another way to help and to give the college a push in the direction a prospect prefers. If development officers know of a tenured professor that a prospect likes or might like, they could suggest the prospect support the professor's research or other activities for a limited duration of time. A larger gift to support this professor might be to establish a permanent fully endowed chair that would allow the college to pay the salary of the professor and perhaps some research support. It could be, for example, the John and Mary Smith Endowed Chair for the Great Books.

Such an endowed chair also guarantees there are funds to hire a future professor in that same field when the former occupant retires. It is a matter of prestige for the professor. It creates a permanent place in the college for that field of studies. An endowed named professorship usually has a lesser price tag than an endowed chair, and may just approximate the salary of the current professor. It is a great boost to the current professor, and it gives the college a fund by which to hire a successor. These gifts have a strategic impact for generations.

If the prospect has a different philosophic or political orientation, really the same principle applies. They too could encourage what they have an interest in. If they had an interest in the environment, they could support a Mary and John Smith Center on the Environmental Sciences, or Gender Studies, and so on as per the examples above. A creative advancement officer should find ways to allow the prospect to support the university in a way that makes both sides happy.

Colleges are pleased to get support for their faculty. These types of gifts affect the types of studies from which students can learn and benefit. No university worth its salt will cede academic governance to a donor pushing a personal agenda. On the other hand, picking and choosing within a framework that allows for a measure of academic freedom in a wide variety of fields is welcome.

Scholarships directly support the students by reducing their expenses. An endowed scholarship gift with naming rights generally requires a hefty amount that can be paid over several years if need be.

Suppose a prospect made a career in the field of chemistry. They could restrict the gift to help students who declare their major in the field of chemistry. Such scholarships could be in any major. A scholarship endowment fund of $1 million might, depending on the college policy, spin off about 5% each year, or $50,000, to assist students in paying their expenses.

Scholarships are often set up simply to help students who are qualified, but who come from families that simply do not have resources to pay the tuition and other expenses. I have seen gifts designed to help students of a certain race or ethnicity. Interestingly, these gifts have been challenged legally in various states since awarding benefits based on race or ethnicity contradict the idea of not discriminating by race. A different approach would be to set up a scholarship fund to attract the most highly qualified students regardless of need. Such a fund would have a strategic value of lifting the academic ranking of the college.

Donors might wish to restrict the awarding of a scholarship by citizenship. Perhaps they wish to restrict support to qualified students of Chinese, Indian, or Nigerian citizenship or some other country where the donor now lives, or from which their ancestors came. Another option would be to restrict the scholarship to students who have American citizenship, or who have served in the United States armed forces. I have worked with a donor to set up a fund to help students who lived in foster-care. These and other options should be explored with prospects.

It takes all kinds to make a successful advancement effort at a university. Advancement officers need to be clear about the needs and priorities of the college. They also need to be aware of what might be of greatest interest to a potential donor. The prospect and the advancement officer may need to get creative and together approach the college about something new. It is also true that money is fungible so that any gift, even those restricted, frees up resources to go elsewhere in the university budget. Still, a restricted gift sends a message and will help the professors and students that a donor may prefer. The bigger the gift, the greater the strategic impact.

THINK TANKS

If a prospect is concerned about the future of America, whether they are of the left or the right, they may wonder why doesn't the President and the Congress do such and such. Let's just take one example: the national debt. The United States has a huge national debt. As I write, it is over 100% of our Gross Domestic Product (GDP). This is the largest amount of debt in relation to GDP since World War II. It looks like it is going to keep increasing for the indefinite future. More than 70% of the current spending is on so-called "mandatory programs" such as Social Security, Medicare, and Medicaid and other programs. That spending will increase unless changes are made.

What should our government do that is best for the common good? Think tanks on the left and the right have very different thoughts on the national debt. Each public policy plan has consequences. Depending on a donor's belief, he might support a think tank that is more along his line of thinking. Raise taxes? Gradually increase age qualification for Social Security? Grow the economy to increase government tax revenue? Cut entitlements? What are the likely consequences to these various approaches? Think tank researchers will make assumptions, tabulate data, search out studies, and pick facts to support their positions. Nonetheless, if they are to remain tax-exempt so that donors can use their gift as a charitable deduction, they can't urge an up or down vote on a specific piece of legislation.

Think tanks, or public policy research organizations, are generally established as non-profit educational and charitable organizations under IRS code 501 C 3. They cannot advocate passage of specific legislation, nor can they support candidates for office. They can gather information, analyze it, and speculate on the consequences of government policies or proposed policies. There are many think tanks, and they depend in great part on donations from the public. Fundraising for these require a certain level of political sophistication as the solicitor tries to make the case for a donation.

The first public policy organization in the United States to my knowledge was The Brookings Institution. It was established in the late 1920s by business leaders who thought the principles of business should be applied to the efficient management of the ever-growing federal government. After the income tax was established in 1913 and after World War I, the federal government began to grow rapidly. The business community still believes it can help government do its job better! Its motives may not always be completely altruistic.

Next came the American Enterprise Institute (AEI), also established by business leaders in the 1940s. This new think tank explored more forthrightly about what policies of government might benefit business and the growth of the economy. Probably the best-known thinker at any of the older think tanks was Herman Kahn. He started the RAND corporation in Southern California after the development of nuclear weapons. Kahn was a genius and one of the leading strategists concerning nuclear war, the escalation of wars, and, as one of his books titles said, *Thinking the Unthinkable*. RAND in its early days received much of its support from the Air Force and various branches of the federal government to help them think through some of the national security implications of their policies. Since then, RAND has spread out its research portfolio, and the sources of its support.

Kahn eventually set up the Hudson Institute on the Hudson River in New York. It then moved to Indianapolis, and it now has offices in Washington, DC. Another of the older guard in the world of think tanks is the Hoover Institution set up in the 1950s by President Herbert Hoover on the campus of Stanford University in California. Originally set up for the "study of war, revolution and peace," it now has a world class archive and formidable scholars in a variety of fields.

The Vietnam War, the ignominious end to the Nixon Presidency, and the related turmoil on the college campuses gave birth from the 1970s to a new wave of think tanks largely based in Washington, DC, and largely conservative. The Heritage Foundation, the Free Congress Foundation, the Ethics and Public Policy Center, The Family Research Foundation, The Cato Institute, Committee for the Clear and Present Danger, Capital Research Center, The Claremont Institute, Manhattan Institute, Heartland Institute, David Horowitz Freedom Center, and many others. Each had their niche. Many of these think tanks morphed, and some grew. The Heritage Foundation, began as a small organization in 1973. Under the leadership of Edwin J. Feulner, it grew to 55 employees by the time I joined it in 1980. It now has well over 200 employees.

There are now many think tanks on the left as well. They saw the significant influences those on the right were having. Some of these include the Center for American Progress, Institute for Policy Studies, Guttmacher Institute, Human Rights Watch, Center on Budget and Policy Priorities, Center for Climate and Energy Solutions, Urban Institute, Worldwatch, People for the American Way, and others.

Some attempt to be "independent" or centrist, though this is a matter for the donor to judge. Some of these include the Center for Strategic and International Studies, Woodrow Wilson International Center for Scholars, Aspen Institute, Freedom House, Council on Foreign Relations, Peter G. Peterson Foundation, and many others

Some of these educational and charitable organizations formed separate 501 C 4 organizations. Unlike their 501 C 3 "cousins," these could lobby and the IRS regulations governing their activities are different. Advancement officers need to be clear as to which organization they are representing, and they need to keep their compensation separate. There is a need to keep a strict separation between the two in terms of their activities and accounting. If not, they may put in jeopardy their tax-exempt status.

Corporations donate to think tanks too. They do it if they believe a given think tank generally advocates positions that line up with their interests. An oil and gas company may support a think tank that publishes a study that says wind and solar are fine, but they should not be heavily subsidized by the federal government. A solar energy company will support a think tank that generally has studies that show how oil and gas are harming the environment, and that solar and wind energy are better. To be persuasive in any of these studies, the author must show a command of empirical data and other studies as well as a clear moral case for why a given policy is best for the common good. Studies that have a conclusion at the outset, and then seek out the facts to justify it, have a place. They may not hold up over time.

Charitable Foundations also support think tanks. It would be nice to think foundations are in some sense politically neutral. In my experience that is generally not the case. The Carnegie Foundation for Peace, the Ford Foundation, the Pew Foundation, and others generally support policy studies of the left. The Koch Foundation, the Lynde and Harry Bradley Foundation, and the William E. Simon Foundation generally support policy studies to the right. This is not to say that any of these policy studies that are directly or indirectly supported by any of these foundations should be disregarded. A study from a think tank that is supported by a given foundation may have such strength that it makes the better case. It may bring to light facts that another study does not. The media may write about it, and that in turn may affect how a member of Congress may decide downstream to vote a decade later on some piece of legislation.

There are some thinkers, like Herman Kahn, who transcend the money trail. OK, maybe the Air Force funded some studies he did. He was of such a stature, that he would do a study that might, or might not, please the people in the Air Force that provided resources for his analysis. It is important that if a donor is thinking to support a public policy think tank, they should look at who else is funding the institution or the study, and they should also have insight into the quality of the individual thinker. A good development officer at a think tank will be helpful in this regard.

Some researchers are very good at both research and writing. They get assigned to one topic or another and crank out studies. There is no question that many of these writers are talented. Nonetheless, they are different than someone who knows the subject and has been immersed in it for years. One of my colleagues who was President of the Howard Center on the Family for many years is Allan Carlson. His Ph. D. thesis was on the social and family planning ideas of Gunnar and Alva Myrdal and the founding of the Swedish welfare state. He did this work in the 1970s. Allan is a brilliant scholar, but he pretty much writes only about the family. He has written, edited, or contributed to about 50 books on the family from the standpoint of social history, theology, economics, cultural history, politics, tax policy, and on and on. He has written on the family wage, welfare, day care, and all sorts of topics on the family. If Allan writes something on the family, you know you are getting what he thinks and concludes. He is not chasing somebody's half-baked trendy idea on what is good public policy as related to the family. The people who have supported Allan's work over the years know this.

The media loves these organizations because they have experts on all manner of subjects with different points of view. If a news reporter for any media organization calls, they can get experts with a point of view to help in the story they are writing. This publicity becomes an arrow in the quiver of the enterprising development officer. If their in-house scholars are frequently cited, it shows impact.

Each of these think tanks depend on donations big and small. They often have aggressive direct mail programs. If a person gives a comparatively small donation to one think tank, it might, in turn, rent their direct mail donor list to another think tank. The donor's mail box may start to get quite full. Raising funds for one of these organizations requires the advancement officer to know its niche in the realm of public policy. By so doing, he can make a better case to a donor. Is the think tank Conservative, Neo-Conservative, Paleo Conservative, Liberal, Libertarian, Classical Liberal, Socialist, Environmentalist, Progressive, etc.? These distinctions can become quite fine. East Coast Straussians are different than West Coast Straussians. Don't ask. In any case, there are donors who prefer one to the other. An effective advancement officer should know the strengths of their organization and the limits of the others.

Further, the challenge in these issue oriented public policy research organizations is to show impact. One way to do it is to count the number of times a study is used in footnotes by other studies. Admittedly that is a boring statistic, but over time such citations carry enormous impact. Another way is to show how many appearances a think tank's experts make on television and radio and the total audience size of each. Another is to count mentions in newspapers and include paid circulation sizes. Social media is a growing way to measure impact in terms of followers, retweets and likes. A picture of the President of the United States looking at a think tank's study and saying he relies on studies from the XYZ think tank would be perfect. That's an audience of one, but in the world of think tanks a statement like that is golden. A donor would get the message that this organization is having impact. It could be the same idea for Senators and members of the House of Representatives in Washington, DC and with their analogues in the fifty states.

SCIENTIFIC RESEARCH

It is quite common to receive requests to support research to abolish cancer or eliminate HIV/Aids. If valid, these gifts would be in most instances considered charitable by the Internal Revenue Service. While ending these diseases and many others is a wonderful goal, the same questions apply as in the case of other charities. How much of a gift goes for scientific research, and how much would go for advertising, fundraising, and administration?

The appeal can be strong because cancer has taken the lives of so many people. If a potential donor has had a death in their immediate family, they may have a greater motivation to give to that cause. Deeply felt emotion can backfire in the face of an over-eager development officer when dealing with a family that has suffered in this way. A profound empathy is required, and it is not the type of attribute that lends itself to goal-oriented pep talks in development meetings.

Sometimes the popular appeals for supporting medical research blur the focus so that it is not clear if the donations go to research or to help patients who have cancer. There is a role for both, but messages need to be clear. The Federal Trade Commission dealt with a more mundane problem a few years back when it ruled that four cancer charities had to return $187 million to the donors. It seems most all the money was used to improve the lifestyles of those who ran the cancer "charities."[14]

How could a potential donor know if the scientific research is cutting edge? The National Science Foundation (NSF) and the Center for Disease Control (CDC) are government agencies whose missions are to support scientific research. These are good starting points. What is the reputation of the organization to which a donor is thinking to fund? Who are the scientists doing the research? Are they working full time for the organization? Or do they have a variety of occupational responsibilities? Do they serve on for-profit pharma boards that are developing related drugs? It is probably well to rely on the NSF and CDC literature for decisions about funding research. If the charity is simply trying to give palliative care for those who suffer from these and other diseases, that is a different matter. Regardless, always due diligence is required.

There are major research efforts going on at the large well established universities like Harvard, Stanford, University of Southern California, University of California at Los Angeles, and other research centers located at universities around the world.

Basic scientific research has led to numerous discoveries that have improved our lives in so many ways. Charitable gift-giving for scientific research requires specialized knowledge, but also full disclosure of any financial interests on the part of the researchers. Development officers needs to know the lay of the land if they expect to succeed in this field. This requires a general knowledge of the major foundations that support research. It also would be helpful to know something of the research itself. In many of these cases, it is the scientist that must become the development officer.

POLITICAL GIVING

Giving in the United States to candidates for political office, to political parties, or to state-wide initiatives and referenda are quite different than charitable giving. While a political campaign for office may be perceived as a cause worthy of support, the motivations for the gifts are quite different than those for making a gift to a non-profit charity. Gifts are not tax deductible. Furthermore, fundraising in the field of politics generally attracts a different type of person than someone who does the same job for non-profits. They are interested in politics to be sure. Fundraisers in this context also have more of a business mentality. Frequently they are part of a for-profit company that specializes in political fundraising, and they may work for several different candidates for different offices at the same time. They need to know well the various candidates in the races and their respective stands on the issues. Without such knowledge, it is hard to persuade a prospect to give. Most of the gifts go toward political advertising.

Candidates

Any donor to candidates running for state office needs to know the details of the state laws that control races for the Governor, any statewide office, or for offices in state Assemblies or Senates. The same holds true for the fundraisers who are asking. The last thing a campaign needs is an investigation into violations of campaign finance law. Laws governing political campaigns for the US Congress, the Presidency, and national parties are different. Each campaign needs to have legal counsel should any questions arise. These laws govern the behavior or donation amounts of a citizen, a company, a union, a political party, or a Political Action Committee (PAC). Why does each state have different laws? It's important to understand.

When the United States was first established by the thirteen colonies, a system of dual sovereignty was set up. The individual states had certain rights, as a sovereign entity, as did the federal government, as a sovereign entity. As an illustrative example, the state motto of Illinois, debated after a bitter Civil War, remained "State Sovereignty; National Union" in that order. There was an effort to change the order, but it failed. Bear in mind this was President Lincoln's home state.

Laws governing political giving change too. For instance, a person could not give more than $2,700 to a campaign for a candidate running in 2016 for the Presidency.[15] For a husband and wife, that would be $5,400. These amounts have changed over the years. In 1968, a donor could give as much as he wanted. There is an important debate to be had about these laws. When Senator Gene McCarthy decided in 1968 to run for the Presidency, he could do so rather quickly because several people gave him gifts that totaled over $1 million. At the time, it was a huge amount of money. He did not have to spend two years traveling the country raising $2,700 per person. Democrat Senator McCarthy took on sitting Democrat President Lyndon Johnson while the Vietnam War raged. His early strong showing was a key factor in President Johnson deciding not to run. There was merit in having unlimited gifts since candidates did not have to spend so much time raising small amounts of money from many sources. On the other hand, with such large donations from a small circle, the question arises about whom the public servant is serving.

In 1974, in the wake of the Presidential election of 1972 in which Richard Nixon won 60.7% of the vote, and in the aftermath of President Nixon's resignation, President Gerald Ford signed into law a bill that limited donations to $1,000 and required disclosure of gifts. The law also limited expenditures by candidates. It was thought that would clean up politics greatly. Later a question was raised about whether the government could limit the amounts spent on campaigns since the law was seen as a limit on free speech and the right to associate with like-minded people. The Supreme Court ruled in 1976 in *Buckley v. Valeo* that expenditure limits were a limit to political speech and a limit to the right to association for political purposes. Limits were challenged under the reasoning the money was equated to freedom of speech. The next milestone in the political donation saga was *Citizens United v. Federal Election Committee* in 2010. The 5-4 ruling of the Supreme Court held that independent corporations, PACs, unions and the like could not be restricted in the amount of their expenditures and the timing. A person could write a check, theoretically, for $100 million to a PAC if the PAC did not co-ordinate with the campaign.

If you find this confusing, join the club. Personally, I would prefer donor disclosure but no limits to gifts to political campaigns. What we have now are PACs run by former campaign aides who know the candidates very well. When a person sees the ad on television, it states in print too small to be read, that the ad was paid for by the XYZ PAC. So, whatever scurrilous things are said, the candidate can say he had nothing to do with it. The ad was created, financed, and placed by free citizens exercising their First Amendment rights. Technically it is true. Nonetheless, the viewer or reader does not always look at the fine print. If these gifts were given directly to the candidate, the voters could more easily hold the candidate accountable for his ads and the conduct of the campaign.

The motivation for these current laws is fine. The consequence is that there are still very wealthy people writing very large checks to all manner of PACs to get candidates they like elected. Often what will happen is that the PAC will put together a host committee to invite other citizens to attend an event in someone's home. The names on that invitation derive from the fundraiser's experience from previous campaigns and from publicly available donor information. The campaign fundraiser or the leader of the PAC asks the potential donors for the required amount for the privilege of being on that invitation. The invitation tells others that these donors are important enough to be on the "inside." The PAC fundraiser will judge how much it might be worth to some wealthy donors to have their name listed on the invitation. To have one's name printed on that Host Committee will require large gifts ranging anywhere from $10,000 to $1 million for a major Presidential candidate. To attend requires a large gift, though not as much as to be on the host committee. The recipient of the invitation looks forward to rubbing shoulders with the rich and powerful and to be part of the effort.

It is possible to have a PAC meeting conducted by the PAC at 5 pm in the home of the event Chair, and then at 6 pm, in that same location, the candidate's campaign could begin a separate meeting. This second meeting will have a separate invitation with a separate Host Committee. The campaign counsel earns his money making these judgment calls about what is the law that governs such things. The dollar amounts in the campaign meeting could not exceed the federal or state limits. Messaging and control for the two meetings are separate. In any case, however much a PAC can raise, the candidate must raise money for his campaign subject to campaign finance rules. That is the money he can use for his campaign.

In a statewide campaign the fundraiser, with candidate in tow, usually must spend several years going around the district, state, or the country speaking and asking people for money. This money will pay for the campaign ads on television, radio, newspapers, the website and social media. It also will pay for staff salaries and the fundraising fees to the fundraiser's company. The company that places the ads typically receive 15% of the value of the ad for the placement. That can be a good amount, and sometimes the fundraising company is full service and creates and places the ads. It's a business.

Another option is that the candidate can donate or lend unlimited amounts to his own campaign. If the candidate is quite wealthy, it makes it difficult for the fundraiser to ask others of much lesser wealth for money. Nonetheless, if that wealthy candidate has a chance of winning, people do like to give to winning candidates and be part of a winning team. That picture on the office wall with the candidate becomes more important. It tells his friends and business associates that he has some pull with the elected official.

Congressmen, once elected, spend time making laws, which is their primary job. Nonetheless, they also must commit to "dialing for dollars" while they are in Washington, DC to raise money for the party. To be in accord with campaign finance law, they cannot do so from their office, so they go to some cubicle across the street in the party headquarters. To ask for gifts while physically in their office is a violation of law. The same is true for state offices. There is a party fundraising team that runs that part of the fundraising operation.

Is there no idealism in political fundraising? It depends. Usually fundraisers are divided by party. They make a career raising money for either Republicans or Democrats. That choice speaks generally to a fundraiser's political beliefs. Nonetheless, there is strong incentive to win the race as it affects the fundraiser's future career. Winning often becomes more important than political philosophy in the mind of the political fundraiser.

In the United States, we have the right and the privilege to vote. Some people are issue voters. Perhaps they believe in a strong national defense and in a candidate who supports that position while another candidate does not want to spend more on defense. Perhaps one is pro-life and another is pro-choice (Pro-life folks refer to this as pro-abortion.). Perhaps one candidate has a position on taxes that a voter likes better than the other. Some people have issues that motivate them to give to candidates that represent their point of view. If a citizen feels strongly about, say, the right to bear arms, they will support that candidate regardless of party. They would give to a candidate based on an issue they think is important. If a citizen lived in California, he could give to a candidate running in Kentucky based on that issue.

Politicians generally are great at trying to be friends with everyone, so the best way to check is to look at their voting record. As is the case of the charities, due diligence is required. Do politicians just follow the money? Usually it doesn't work that way. The money generally will flow toward a politician that a person or group feels will be sympathetic to their views. These are not sure things, and some politicians are brilliant at seeming to agree with all sides on an issue. Donors and voters must pay attention.

Some donors have more of a self or business interest involved in the matter. They are not so much driven by an issue. They like to buy access. I once knew a high-ranking executive in Las Vegas who was a conservative Republican who supported Democrat Harry Reid for the US Senate representing Nevada. I asked the executive why. I was told that their company had been supporting the Senator for years and if they had an issue, his door was always open. The challenger would likely lose and they had much money invested in the sitting Senator. If they needed a clause in a tax bill that would benefit their industry, they could call the Senator. No point in calling the loser.

Some people, of course, give because of a mix of issues and interests. It is often hard to draw clear lines separating motivations. At a fund-raising event where the candidate is available for conversation or a picture, it is a thrill for some donors. If you are a Very Important Person and give at a certain level, you may qualify to have your picture taken with the candidate. This is the standard transaction. That picture might later appear on a piano in a person's home, or on a wall in their office, so visitors can know immediately that he is a Very Important Person. Of course, if a person has pictures with Mayors, US Representatives, US Senators, the Governor, and the President, well, you get the idea. VVIP. If candidates visit this person's office, they too are immediately thinking they better pay attention to this person who likely has donated to these many other elected officials.

What about ethics? When these questions come up, I often think of the opening scene in the Coen brothers movie, *Miller's Crossing*. The gangster is reasoning aloud about an ethical problem. It seems he paid a fighter to take a dive in a certain round, and he didn't take the dive. It is a certain kind of ethical problem. The gangster set about solving it in the usual way gangsters do. Long time Speaker of the California Assembly, the legendary Willie Brown, reputedly said one time that a person shouldn't be in politics if they couldn't take money from a donor and then turn around and, forgive me, "screw 'em." What he may have implied is that a donor can't really buy a politician worth his salt. A good politician should vote for the common good even though a donor would prefer he not. Well, that is one interpretation. Or, it could be that another donor who had a different interest gave much more. Politicians are generally in office because they are good enough at mastering the political arts. There are good reasons these gifts are not tax deductible.

INITIATIVES AND REFERENDA

Initiatives and referenda are a bit different. These began to gain currency in the early 1900s at the outset of the "Progressive Era." In theory, initiatives arose from citizens who believed that their elected representatives were not responsive to their concerns. At that time, it was believed by many that business moguls often controlled politicians. A citizen initiative could place a referendum on the ballot and citizens could directly vote on the matter and bypass their elected representatives. The politicians would be bound by the popular vote of citizens.

Again, the laws and regulations that control initiatives that lead to popular referenda varies by states where they are part of the political process. Counties can do it too. In California, a donor can give as much as they like to an organization backing a proposition that will raise taxes; limit marriage to a man and a woman; give the state the authority to issue a bond; legalize marijuana; or ban plastic bags. There is no tax deduction allowed for these donations.

Before the initiative process gets rolling, often a core group will hire a polling company to test if it has a chance of winning. Who pays for that? It is that small core group of people who feel that the initiative is important. They may test certain wordings to see what works best. If the effort has a possibility of success, the campaign must collect the required number of signatures to qualify for a listing on the ballot. The laws governing the process, again, vary by state. Companies specialize in obtaining signatures go to work and they are paid by the number of signatures gathered. They usually collect well over the required amount as the bona fides of the signatures might be challenged. After all, is Donald Duck really a registered voter?

The wording of the referendum that appears on the ballot goes through a legal process to make sure it reflects accurately what it would do. Once accepted for the ballot by the appropriate government agency, the fundraising begins in earnest. And then, "let the games begin!" All the entities, pro and con, can spend millions of dollars advocating or opposing the referendum. The people decide. California with its 40 million people has made the initiative process a highly-developed industry. A referendum will have a campaign staff to create press releases and television ads, send out mailers, and hire spokespersons to champion the cause. Originally the idea was to give the people an option, if their elected officials in the state capitol were not responsive to them. Sometimes the elected leaders like these propositions since they then do not have to be held accountable for the outcome. The forces opposing the referendum gear up in similar fashion.

Though there is a leadership core at the outset of the initiative process, there is need to hire fundraisers to raise additional money. Depending on the issue, fundraisers need to ferret out who might have an interest in the outcome of the vote. If the referendum is about a definition of the family, fundraisers will go to those who have supported religiously oriented causes in the past. Some elected politicians or candidates may jump in. Those opposing will seek out supporters of gay rights. Or, it may be that a referendum has environmental implications or energy implications. The fundraiser will go after supporters of those related issues. If potential donors are asked to give to support a certain statewide proposition, they should be careful. What may seem right and plain common sense doesn't matter if you are outspent five to one and there are some clever commercials. In California alone over $473 million was raised for various initiatives in 2016.[16] The people who ask citizens to support an initiative, very often leave out facts or likely consequences. Public employee unions, industry unions, businesses, industry associations, public utilities, political parties, and the rest all have interests in the outcome. Tobacco and pharmaceutical companies were the largest contributors to initiatives in California in 2016 with $153 million.[17]

When fundraisers ask a prospect to give, they need to know clearly the issue and its likely implications as well as who is supporting it; who is opposing it; and why they oppose it. They also need to be able to explain the case for his side persuasively. As is true in most any context, if a fundraiser asks another to give, they should believe in the cause and have made at least a token gift. The people who raise the most money in these more political of causes generally have given the most. Sometimes a fundraiser simply needs to work with that donor to find others and to schedule phone calls or meetings.

VENTURES

There is another type of fundraising known to investors. A person has an idea for a business and seeks support for a first round of fundraising to do an initial launch. Perhaps the person is connected to the scientific faculty and researchers at a university and comes across some scientific research that they believe could lead to a product or invention that could benefit many and which could be sold for profit. Obviously, the request for funds is for an investment. It is not a gift. The investor is looking for a return. No tax deduction. Nonetheless, I mention it here because the founder or pioneer generally has passion and makes this venture a cause. These types of requests for funding necessarily involve high risk. There are so many questions to be answered. Unless possible investors are professionals with a track record, and unless they are prepared to lose it all, they should steer clear.

More recently, universities do get into the act with these types of ventures. If it is their research that is being used for a product, even if developed as part of their non-profit mission, a university might reap some reward. Suppose a professor or a venture makes a product derived from university research that goes to market and enjoys great success. Different universities have different policies regarding these matters. Often the university will demand a cut of the ownership, or profit, for any research developed that leads to a company making a profit. If you are the type of person who is an entrepreneur, and if you wish to encourage such at your alma mater or the nearby college or university, you might be interested to explore and negotiate the matter. The legal boundary between profit and not-for-profit need careful attention in these matters.

There is another type of pitch that is used by, frankly, crooks. Of course, Ponzi is the classic example but Bernie Madoff is a more recent one. The people who fall prey to these con artists and others can be highly intelligent and accomplished people. I won't list notables on Mr. Madoff's list of dupes. They have suffered enough. Nonetheless, ask yourself how could a Noble Prize recipient fall prey to such schemes? Usually, the victims are made to feel that they are special and part of an elite fortunate group that is getting in on something that ordinary people simply would not come across. The adage that "if something sounds too good to be true, then likely it is,' applies. Similarly, if someone says "it" is a sure thing, that is the time that your acute danger radar should be activated. Third party verification is needed. Track records need to be carefully analyzed. But, that's enough on this type of request for funds.

CHAPTER III

Some Strategic Considerations

THE WILL

L ET'S START WITH SOME BASICS when a potential donor first begins to think seriously about making a significant gift. Before giving thought to charitable gifts, a potential donor should have a will. Even if people do not wish to do anything for charity, they should have a will. It is surprising how many people do not have one. Admittedly, it is not pleasant to contemplate death. Many would rather not. They figure they will get to it later. While there are few things more certain than one's own death, the precise expiration date is unknown. Stories abound of celebrated cases of wealthy famous people who die without a will. Picasso is one. While a great artist, he did not burden himself much with morality and the law. He had multiple wives and affairs and children from both. He had many paintings. If later in life he drew something on a napkin at a restaurant, it had, and has, great value. Rather than make a will, which admittedly would be quite complicated in his case, he died in 1973 at the age of 91. He died, as they say, intestate. No will. It caused legal and personal battles that endure to this day. You might say, "What does he care? He is dead." No problems. Well, no problems for him. He did, however, leave many angry and disappointed people, and they were those who were closest to him.

In the United States, if people have assets and die without a will, the state presides over the distribution of their assets and charges a fee for the service. Of course, there are laws on the books generally deciding who gets what, but as with all things human, it can be quite complicated. Most people would not want strangers deciding who gets what and charging a fee. Not good. Besides, each state has different rules for deciding who gets what. So, at the least, people can go to the Internet and find LegalZoom where they can follow procedures to create a simple will at comparatively little expense. If people are not destitute, they should find an attorney who specializes in estate planning. The remaining family will still go through probate, and the state will take a cut. Nonetheless, the deceased will make the call in the matter of who gets what. In California, the probate fees today are 4% on the first $100,000 with a declining percentage as the assets increase. When you reach $800,000, it is 1% for each dollar more, and so on.[18] Again, these amounts vary by the state. In addition, a will and probate is a public event. The whole world can look it up and learn who has gotten what.

If people are so fortunate as to have an estate greater than the $5.45 million, they really should hire an estate attorney who knows well estate and tax laws. While that $5.45 million escapes the estate tax, commonly called the death tax, each dollar after that as I write in 2017 is taxed at 40%. Many excellent attorneys have little idea of the intricacies of estate planning and laws. It isn't just the approximately 98,000 pages in the IRS regulations. It is also that the US Congress adds each year to the laws. The IRS dutifully then translates these into regulations. However bright attorneys are in mergers and acquisitions or commercial real estate, they may not have a clue about estate planning law. Even when a person hires an attorney to create a will, it often happens that the estate attorney may simply follow what they understand is the clients wishes. What people with substantial assets should have is an estate attorney who can help them think through what is best when considering the client's values, assets, family, other business interests, insurance, and the like.

Experienced senior advancement officers at a larger philanthropic organization may have some ideas that they have picked up along the way. Even so, if prospects have estates more than the Unified Estate Tax Exemption of $5.45 million, they need professional advice to maximize what is kept for their family and their other interests, including charity.

A larger charity usually will have a stable of outside attorneys, CPAs, Certified Financial Planners (CFPs), and insurance agents who are knowledgeable about estate planning. The advancement officer with whom a potential donor is dealing should be able to provide a list from which a donor prospect might choose. Some staff attorneys employed by the charity will perform these services at no expense if the charity is tucked in to the list of beneficiaries. An experienced advancement officer will understand that a prospect may have a variety of charitable interests. Usually these attorneys are reputable as it is in the charity's interest that it be so. In an abundance of caution, and perhaps when the estate is quite large, it would be wise for a donor to have their own attorney. The reason is simple enough. If grandma leaves $10 million to some charities and a very small amount to family heirs, these heirs might allege in a law suit that the attorney and the charity took advantage of grandma when she was not of sound mind. In either case, it is well that grandma lets her heirs know at least her general plans while she is of sound mind. The heirs need to be satisfied that is the case. These estate tussles require that the charities bend over backwards to make sure the highest standards of professional integrity are observed.

THE LIVING TRUST

Better than a will, in my view, is a living trust. It is generally a little more expensive than a will in terms of the up-front costs, but it saves on the back end (The back end is, er, death.). Assets in a living trust bypass the expense of probate. So, a person's assets should be kept within the trust whether it be a house, a savings account, or other such assets. As mentioned above, these can add up. Unlike going through probate, a living trust keeps the distribution of assets private. Further, it gives a person more control. If a person becomes mentally incompetent due to

The family members meet quarterly to decide what charities they wish to support. They now get requests each year from many charities. So, they have decided that they are only going to give to certain specified areas. They put up on their website what these areas are and what they require from the charities that make the requests. Joe and Mary like giving to conservatively oriented free-enterprise public policy research organizations. They require the most recent 990 form and an audited financial statement in every request. This cuts down on the number of requests that come in. By law they must give away about 5% of their assets each year or they must pay federal taxes on the difference.[24]

Joe and Mary are happy because they are "giving back" and because they are teaching their children the importance of free-enterprise and charity. They have enjoyed tax advantages. They added a few of their friends on the Board of Trustees who think the way they do. Fast forward 30 years. Joe and Mary have passed away and have left another $50 million to their foundation. Their friends who served on the Board also have either passed away or retired from the Board. The original $25 million has become $50 million through prudent investing. John and Sara have asked several of their friends to join the Board because the state in which they operate requires at least three people, and they wanted their business acquaintances or friends on the Board. Further, it turns out that John likes environmental causes and Sara really wants to focus on helping the disabled. So, they change the by-laws and the giving priorities with the approval of their board members. They now have $100 million to manage and give away about $5 million each year. They hire a President, program officer, and a bookkeeper to manage the assets, evaluate proposals, and disperse the grants. You can see how over time the agenda of the foundation can change.

Joe and Mary are rolling over in their graves. What could they have done differently? They had by-laws. They had a stated purpose. I know the example of one foundation that built in a self-destruct plan. After the death of the founder who was Chairman of the Board, the charity had twenty years to give away all the assets. The founding Chairman picked his successor before he died, and he picked his board members who thought the way he thought in terms of national defense, free-enterprise, and welfare reform. With the death of the founding Chairman, the foundation had twenty years to give away all the foundation assets. In this way, he could be assured that the foundation would remain true to its original purpose. In the end, it would no longer exist. On the other hand, Joe and Mary both passed on believing the money they put into the foundation was going to go to support the causes they liked. It didn't turn out that way.

There are numerous stories of such foundations "going bad" after the founder passes away. The purpose of the foundation, especially when the amounts of money involved are large, may change and the types of charities supported might change from what the founders wished. No matter how precise the founding language, this can happen in one or two generations. New board members come on the Board of Trustees, and a President, hired by the Board, may have some other ideas. It is true that needs change. An organization set up in the 1930s to ensure international communism does not take over the world really is not helping society very much today. There have been celebrated cases where the founders vision is turned on its head. The Ford Foundation and the J. Howard Pew Freedom Trust come to mind.

DONOR ADVISED FUNDS

If people do not wish to set up a foundation, nor worry about filing with the federal government, hiring a staff, managing the assets, evaluating proposals, and making sure it gives away the 5% of the assets, they could set up a donor advised fund (DAF). Most large mutual funds will give people this option and so will local community foundations and larger charities. It is especially attractive for people who have an exceptionally large income in a given year.

The donors simply give the stocks or cash to the DAF along with general guidance as to the types of things to be supported. The donor receives the benefit of the charitable deduction in the year the assets are delivered to the institution that manages the DAF. The DAF becomes part of the filing requirement of the charity or mutual fund that hosts it, so there is no federal filing burden on the donor. The act of giving the money to the DAF allows the tax deduction and it can be up to 50% of the Adjusted Gross Income for a person in a given year with the five year carry over, or 30% if the gift is an appreciated asset. Donors can set the parameters of the giving intent and can also direct the fund to make specific gifts to specific organizations. The host must perform due diligence to make sure the recommended charity is legitimate and then will follow through with the gift. There is the possibility that the host won't do as the donor advises if they find a problem with the proposed organization. This rarely happens because the host would like donors to contribute more so they could manage more assets.

The fee structures vary and donors should examine them with care. They are low when compared to the time and cost it would take to establish and manage a foundation. A reputable DAF fund might require a minimum contribution of $25,000 to begin and charge .5% for an annual management fee. Some charge less. It is always good to shop around. Any capital gains increase in the principal is tax free to the donors. As the DAF increases through additional contributions or the growth of principal, the fees go down as a percentage. If the donors to the DAF direct the host to make the gift, they could direct it to make the gift in the name of the DAF or the host fund, if the donors wish to keep their identity more private.

As is true with most anything involving taxes, the specific rules regarding DAFs can change and there are organizations and associations in Washington, DC that always seek to change laws. So, donors need to pay attention! DAFs can also be set up for successors to the original contributors to direct the host fund for charitable gift giving.

DAFs are becoming increasingly popular. In 2014 there were 238,293 of these, whereas in 2010 there were 184,364. Charitable assets grew in that time frame from $33.6 billion to $70.7 billion.[25]

Large Foundations and universities are starting to host DAFs as well. Donors can, if they wish, sunset their DAFs to avoid the problem of a change in the vision upon their death.

The Bequest

Many people simply want to leave a bequest to a charity or charities. When they pass on, they leave gifts from their estate. It can be done by a specific amount or a percentage. They could leave 5% of their estate to one charity, 5% to another, and another 5% to yet another. At the time the will is drawn up on a percentage basis, no one can say what the amount will be. Others may prefer to name a specific amount, like $100,000, rather than a percentage. Obviously, any non-profit would be delighted to receive in the mail a letter from the estate with a check. If the amount is large, and if it for a specific purpose, it would be good for the charity to know in advance as it can be incorporated into their planning process.

I knew a very successful investor, let's call him Winston, who refused to make an endowed gift to a non-profit because he compared his investment returns to the investment returns of the non-profit. Being facile with numbers, he reasoned that after seven years he could double his money whereas the endowment of the non-profit would only increase the endowment gift by 50%. Who could argue with that reasoning?

Well, there are some other considerations. No one can predict the future. As any novice investor knows, past investment performance is no guarantee of future performance. Still the prospect might feel he could outperform the endowment fund of a given charity. Nonetheless, the charity to which the future donor plans to give his bequest, could do much good in the ensuing seven years. It is also true that the donor could die in a few years. Donors do not have expiration dates. How many people could his gift have helped in the meantime? What new scientific research could be developed if the gift were given? How many future leaders could be prepared to solve nagging human problems? How many others, who are thinking of giving a gift, would be encouraged to follow Winston's example in gift giving because they trust Winston? Then too, Winston could perhaps lend his expertise and talents to the charitable endeavor while he is alive and make his gift have greater impact. Though it may not be quite as charitable in motivation, Winston would have many grateful people who appreciate him while he is alive. He would be part of something greater than himself. It is the idea that it is more blessed to give than receive. There is much to be said for the fellowship and comradery enjoyed from pulling together to help others. So, there are opportunity costs in waiting until the funeral to make your gift.

A Conundrum

Many wealthy people are reluctant to set up a foundation for fear that it will go bad. I gave examples earlier in the section on foundations. At the same time, some folks are reluctant to make large capital or endowment gifts to charities for fear that the charity will go bad. They also would prefer not to "donate" the money to the government, because governments are notoriously inefficient and ineffective. In fact, most people spend a great deal of time and effort seeking to deprive the government of all claims on their wealth through taxes. This leaves only two options. One is to leave what they can to their children. Admittedly few of us have estates greater than the amount currently exempted by the federal estate tax. That is now at this writing about $5.45 million. Nonetheless, let's say Victor, whose wealth does exceed the exemption amount, wants to leave everything in his estate to his children. He is willing to pay the 40% to the government. He can live with government possibly going bad. As mentioned, governments in the best of circumstances are not known to be efficient and effective in how they spend money. It is Victor's money, so why not? But then the question arises in a new form: what is to prevent his heirs from going bad?

History is filled with the stories of wealthy families leaving fortunes to their children who then dissipate it in one or two generations. The children have no incentive to get the most out of their God-given talents. Why get A's in school or be a super achiever at whatever they spend their time at? They lack any financial incentive to make themselves useful to society. Do they have true friends or a loving spouse, or do they have people who associate with them in the hope of gaining some sort of benefit derived from the inherited wealth? In short, a wealthy person's heirs can go bad too.

The same is true of a person's business or his investments. Give the stocks and ownership interests back to the businesses? Not a bad thing, of course. But who is to say the next generation of leadership in that business group will carry on with the entrepreneurial spirit, prudence, and drive of the previous generations? They may fail or just sell the company.

Some families develop elaborate plans with a family constitution and a family office to mitigate the dissipation of the family wealth and to leave a legacy for generations. They will hire specialists to work diligently to develop rules and metrics for deciding who runs certain businesses; how the wealth is to be invested; and, yes, a place for philanthropy as well. It is all well and good. It does provide a way for the coming generations of family members to have incentives to achieve and to be vital members of their communities. Nonetheless, as has been shown, from the standpoint of the donor, foundations can go bad; a charity can go bad; and the next generation of family members can go bad too. It is the human condition. So, it is time in this little treatise to consider those non-profit charitable organizations who depend upon souls with the ability and inner motivation to donate to a good cause. If a person has wealth to spare, certainly a viable option to consider is giving something to a charity that has a vital mission, a proven track record, and an excellent dedicated leadership.

CHAPTER IV

The Gift and
the Group

Most any **CEO** of any non-profit organization would love to have an enormous gift with no restrictions required by the donor. While possible, in today's world that is increasingly unlikely. If the gift is small, it is virtually impossible to direct or restrict it to one specific facet of a non-profit. If the organization solicits people through the mail, and they respond with a comparatively smaller gift (say anything up to $1,000), the donor has little control over how that money will be spent by the non-profit. It's a matter of trust. These types of gifts just get plugged in to whatever the leadership judges to be the key immediate priorities for the organization. They may have hot button issues that elicit the gift, but it really doesn't matter. Think of it this way. The organization has limited resources. They want that solicitation to have the highest rate of return, so that more resources can go to support their work. If they go through a detailed description of a specific project, and the return on the mailing is poor, it is a waste of resources.

A hypothetical case of the Red Cross illustrates dramatically the problem. Say there is a tremendous flood disaster in Florida. The Red Cross will immediately respond locally, regionally, and even nationally to provide emergency services to those in need from a major disaster. It is what they do. They may go on television to solicit support, but regardless of the response to the television ad, the Red Cross is already in motion to save lives. Money in the next few weeks pours in. A month later, much of the immediate need is over. So, the Red Cross saves whatever money they have for the next disaster. People gave at the time of the terrible disaster in Florida, but when in California there is a monster fire with people burned out of their homes, the national Red Cross may support the local affiliate with some of the money it received during the previous Florida disaster. When a person gives to the non-profit in such a manner, he is saying that he trusts the organization to make the best use of the gift.

For larger gifts, a donor may wish to be very specific and contractual. I know of a rare case where a very wealthy person in the construction business wanted to make a gift to alma mater to build an athletic complex. He stated the amount he would give and he named the company that would build it for that price. He also controlled major decisions about seating, concession stands, and many details. That was the deal. It was a gift. It was made in good faith. The size of the gift was huge; the price for the stadium was a bargain; and the donor derived no personal benefit. He just believed that he could build the facility much more efficiently than the university could. Probably the big donors to the university knew the need. In fact, it likely that the university asked this donor to make a lead gift for a multi-year campaign to raise the money; participate in endless committee meetings involving people who knew little about construction, but wanted a say in the color of the seats; and then go through a construction bidding process that would result in a price greater than this donor would arrange. Interestingly, this donor specifically did not want the facility named after him. It is a fabulous facility completed in record time. The university stepped back and let the donor use his wealth and expertise to advance the university. Not all universities would do that, since it cedes a degree of institutional control outside the normal way of operating.

Most large gifts are somewhere in between. A thoughtful and wealthy donor may see a need in the organization that the organization has not seen. The organization has a list of priorities that were developed through a strategic planning process. The Board of Directors and the President have signed off on it. To accept a very large gift for something not on that list is not to be done lightly. Usually such donors will want a signed contract.

Suppose a church has a building plan. Nowhere in the plan is a line item for a new organ. The donor loves music. He believes that a new high quality organ will inspire parishioners. The donor wants to make a very generous gift to his church. He sees something that the pastor and church leadership did not see. This is an instance where the donor may wish to have a contract that says he will give a certain amount of money for a new organ. The authorized head of the church corporation signs it. The donor gives; the church needs to deliver. If not, there may be legal exposure and the donor might demand his gift back.

Perhaps the most celebrated case of a disputed gift contract involved Princeton University and the heirs to the A & P grocery empire.[26] To recap, the A & P was a very large and successful grocery chain, founded in 1859 as the Great Atlantic and Pacific Tea Company. The A & P, as it came to be known, had over 15,000 locations at its peak. The heirs to the A & P fortune gave Princeton University a $35 million endowment gift in 1961. It was agreed by contract that the fund would be used permanently to educate students at their graduate Woodrow Wilson School of Public and International Affairs to be future foreign service officers for the US State Department. In 2002, 41 years later, the children of the original donors sued Princeton to return the money since, according to the suit, Princeton did not use the money for that purpose. The heirs alleged that the resources were not used properly, and that the original gift was now worth $900 million due to the growth in the endowment fund set up back in 1961. Eventually there was a reported settlement with Princeton keeping most of the money. Nonetheless, they paid $40 million in legal fees that the heirs had incurred and returned about $60 million to the family's foundation. This whole chain of events occurred over many years and caused terrible publicity for Princeton. There was obviously much personnel turnover at Princeton from the time of the gift. But then, there was the matter of the contract.

In retrospect, the generous gift from the donors in 1961, though well-intentioned, was not well crafted. It was just too narrow. The US Foreign Service now accepts about 3% of those who apply. Even Princeton graduates might not make it. Then too, the US State Department has a logic of its own as to where its mid-career officers might study. This case is a cautionary tale for both givers and receivers. If a donor makes an endowed gift with narrow language, the charity that receives it must abide by the contract. Yet, suppose the stated purpose has no takers? The money would just sit in the account. In this case, likely it would have been better if the university would have taken note of the problem early on. The President might have gotten back in touch with the donors to review options while the people involved were still around.

Easy for me to say after more than fifty years! Who knows what the exact conversations were that surrounded the agreement? If there can be no true agreement between the donor and the recipient, it is better not to take the gift. That is an advancement challenge! The case of Princeton also illustrates a further problem. As time goes by and the donor, the President and the advancement officers who signed the contract pass on, the institutional memory grows hazy. The money is there, why not use it for some new urgent need??

Another example, though a little less dramatic, illustrates a different problem. Suppose a donor contributes to an organization's endowment. The agreement, or contract, is drawn up and George and Naomi Jones contribute a generous $1 million endowment gift to an organization. They wanted to make sure the organization is on a sound footing and is not a fly-by-night organization. They think this will give the organization staying power. So, to compliment the annual gifts the organization receives along with the multi-year grants, they contribute to the permanent endowment for a certain purpose. Say the gift is to support the publications department. It means that the publications program is to be a permanent part of the organization. Fast forward a few years later, and, low and behold, this fine organization cannot make payroll.

What to do? Well, there is that money in the endowment that just sits there spinning off its 5% each year to give the organization staying power and support publications. But the organization sure would like to take a good chunk of the endowment to make payroll. An emergency meeting of the Board is called and the CEO explains what he has in mind. A board member, Joyce Kiljoy, is an attorney who specializes in non-profit law. She points out that such an action would be a violation of the contract with George and Naomi to set up a permanent endowment for publications. Not only would George and Naomi be very upset to learn about this, they may tell others that the organization isn't trustworthy.

What is required is for the CEO, with the Board's permission, to go to George and Naomi, and get their written permission to borrow, say, 50% from their gift to the endowment fund. They also need to have any terms and conditions spelled out for the loan such as possible interest rates and a timetable to repay. Perhaps George and Naomi, who like the organization and the CEO, will not be too onerous on interest payments and date of repayment. But, surely, they will want to know what the plan is to get the organization back on its feet with its publications program intact. The Board and the CEO need to be focused. They are in crisis.

Say a few more years go by, and that endowment fund remains cut in half. Staff has been cut. Not only is that endowment gift down by 50%, but some others are as well. Let's say that despite the Board's best good faith effort and that of the CEO, the ship continues to leak. What then? In these dire circumstances, after all strategies and tactics are tried to no avail, the organization should consider folding. The CEO needs to go to all living supporters who have set up an endowment fund, and have a heart to heart talk. Whatever assets are left might be given to another non-profit tax-exempt organization that has a similar mission. It happens. In fact, I have seen that language in the articles of incorporation where a specific successor organization is already named in case of such an eventuality. That is why donors, before making a gift to a permanent endowment fund or a long-term multi-year gift, need to do their homework. Look at that 990 form. Check on the Board. Evaluate the CEO. Donors should be satisfied that the organization is viable and has a future. They should make sure that all understand that the gift to the endowment fund is from then on intrinsic to the life of the organization. Once the gift is made, it is a done deal.

In dealing with donors, especially wealthy donors that can make very large gifts, not only the President but the Chief Development Officer, need to be quite conscious of their fiduciary responsibility to the major donors. These very large endowment gifts are thrilling and a time of great excitement. They also require a seriousness on the part of the non-profit to deliver in perpetuity their side of the agreement. Non-profit corporations of this nature are designed to outlive those who give and those who receive.

Chapter V
Charitable Agreements

Estate Planning

THERE IS NO WAY AROUND IT. Serious advancement officers need to understand the basics about estate planning and planned gifts. Of course, so should donors, especially if they have a considerable amount of wealth. If done properly, planned gifts can be a powerful way to help a donor's heirs and charity. The loser is the federal government. If advancement officers have only a vague understanding of estate planning, it would be in the interest of the charity to send them to such a training session.

Many years ago, I took several seminars from a company that teaches advancement officers about "planned gifts." I still use what I learned from it. R.R. Newkirk out of Chicago does a good job. They have experts who teach advancement officers at different levels of knowledge in their professions. In addition to presenting the basics, they guide attendees through exercises to fill out test examples of what planned gifts will do for the donor's taxes. Crescendo Interactive is another. Crescendo offers teaching conferences, and also has software to help make projections to show the tax implications of an estate plan. The software should keep up with the ever-changing tax code. If the non-profit is thinking long-term, it is an investment that will pay dividends over the years. It is a longer-term proposition, but the sizes of the gifts are much larger than typical annual gifts.

PLANNED GIFTS

Planned gifts generally work for supporters that have a comparatively high net worth, appreciated assets, and are further along in the life cycle. These are for people who really do like a specific non-profit tax-exempt organization, or several organizations, and want to make a lasting difference. It generally is not good to be aggressive with these types of gifts since they are serious and very personal. Most organizations will make their donors aware of these different ways of giving through an in-house ad in their publications or perhaps an occasional mailing of a personal letter and brochure. The organization, if it is large, will have an in-house attorney who has expertise in these areas. Unlike a will or living trust, these types of gifts have current tax and income implications for the donor and the charity and have an effect on the estate. Estate planning attorneys often have expertise in these areas as well, but not necessarily. If the charity does not have qualified attorneys on staff, it should have qualified attorneys in their network whom they trust. It would be good if the non-profit suggested several different options of experts from which a donor could pick. Any reputable attorney should fully disclose who is paying for his time if it a matter of a referral. If the organization is paying the attorney, it needs to disclose it and advise the donor of their interest and the interests of the charity. If donors pay the attorneys, there is no question whose interests they are serving. I have found that in-house attorneys are fine for the donor, and they will draw up the documents at no expense if the donor is planning to include the charity in the plan. It need not be an exclusive interest, as charities do recognize a donor may like several different charities.

Because these gifts are larger and because they effect the estate of a person, it is best for the charity to bend over backwards when it comes to being scrupulous. That is the way to avoid being sued by a disgruntled heir who feels short changed in the disposition of an estate. As mentioned, if done properly the heirs and the charity both benefit. The government is the loser. Here follow some common types of planned gifts.

CHARITABLE GIFT ANNUITY (CGA)

When I first learned about charitable gift annuities, I thought they were too good to be true. It seemed like something a con man would present. My wariness radar lit up due to my ignorance. There are some serious reasons why a CGA might make sense for a donor and benefit the charity.

Suppose Nancy, age 75, told Ron she really wanted to help her college, but she was not able to give the whole $100,000 in the previous example. The ever-resourceful Ron asks if she ever considered a CGA. Nancy had no idea what that was. Ron says if Nancy gave all the 1,000 shares now worth $100,000 but purchased for $10,000, she would by-pass the capital gains tax, and the college would pay her 5.8%, or $5,800 a year, for the rest of her life. The kicker was that Nancy would get a sizable tax deduction for such a gift. How much? Well, the actual precise dollar amount depends on how old Nancy is and other aspects of her estate. In fact, her age would also determine the annuity rate. The older you are, the greater the charitable tax deduction and the higher the annuity payment rate. Nowadays, these rates are much better than the current rate for certificates of deposits from the banks. When Nancy dies, the college would keep whatever was left of that $100,000 that they have been investing.

The American Council on Gift Annuities is the gold standard for determining interest rates for CGAs. Rates change depending on actuarial tables about life expectancy and the general condition of markets. If you are 90 years old, you would get a higher interest rate and a larger charitable tax deduction. The rates vary but now it likely would be around 9%. Odds are good a donor of that age is not going to be living too much longer, and the charity is going to get a larger amount. Having written that, I know of a man who died when he was well over 100 years old. He started in his mid-90's making charitable gifts through a series of CGAs. He received great tax deductions. Pay-out rates at one point hit 10% as I recall. He enjoyed beating the actuarial tables. If a husband and wife were 70, in 2017, it might be about 5%. Since the charity keeps whatever is left in the above example, Nancy's children would not receive any of it. That is a downside. Nancy would be wise to tell any heirs about what she is doing while mentally competent. She should also tell them that by-passing capital gains tax and getting a charitable deduction right now, there would be a later benefit to her estate for her children.

Insurance companies sell annuities, and the rates are a little better. The difference is there is no charitable deduction. That tax deduction helps preserve part of the donor's estate since less money goes to the government in taxes. Another consideration is that Nancy would be locked in at a fixed rate for life. Suppose interest rates and inflation go way up. I do recall in the early 1980s a one year $100,000 certificate of deposit (CD) could get 18% from a bank. I was buying them for a non-profit at the time, and we were worried that if we locked in at 18%, we would miss out on the 19% rate that might appear the next month! It sounds unbelievable today. Also, if inflation is 8% a year or higher for a long time, locking in to 5.8% on an annuity is going to reduce the value of those dollars over the years. Interest rates and inflation have been low for such a long time. No one knows when interest rates will increase. They will sometime and so will inflation.

Donors, who are also investors, should have a diversified portfolio of investments to protect themselves against contingencies as they make their estate plans. A charitable gift annuity is often a very good thing for a part of that plan, and it is simple. Of course, the charity should honor the commitment to make those payments. Can it? The donor should check out their 990 form, the audited financial statement, the Board of Directors, the President, and all the other things mentioned earlier. Good advancement officers should be knowledgeable about this aspect of the organization. If the charity has a good track record, then a donor could conclude that even if the market went down, and even if the donor lived much longer than every actuarial table showed, that annuity payment would be honored. As risks go, it is not bad. It is wise to see if the non-profit has sizable assets on which to draw in case there is a dramatic market downturn.

Charitable Remainder Uni-Trust (CRUT)

There are other instruments in the planned giving tool kit. One of the most popular is the Charitable Remainder Uni-Trust (CRUT). Suppose Harriet, age 77, owns 10,000 shares of ABC, Inc. stock that she purchased years ago for $10 a share and it is now worth $100 a share. She paid $100,000 and the stock is now worth $1 million. If she sold the stock, she would have to pay a capital gains tax on the $900,000. Harriet did not want to do a gift annuity because she was worried about inflation. Her mother lived to 100 and she was also planning to live to 100. If the value of a dollar declined dramatically and inflation sky rocketed, she would be locked in at something like 5.8%. Harriet was meeting with Sarah, the experienced advancement officer assigned to her. She told her of a CRUT, and how it could work to protect her from inflation.

If Harriet gave the 10,000 shares to alma mater for an endowment gift, she would not suffer any capital gains tax. That is a huge benefit since paying tax on a $900,000 gain is quite a bit of money. If Harriet were single and her taxable annual income was less than $400,000, as I write this today she would pay 15%, or $135,000. Also, since the amount of the tax deduction was large, she might be able to carry over some of the charitable deduction for as much as the next five years. It would not all be used up in that initial year. The university would take the assets and invest them as part of their endowment fund, taking care that her portion was always accounted for. As the endowment grew, so would Harriet's CRUT. Sarah told her she could pick the payout rate with the minimum being 5% of the invested amount. That would be $50,000 a year. But, she could choose 6% or even 7%. Naturally people would want more, but there would be tax consequences. The higher the pay-out rate, the less charitable deduction. Suppose the fund only earned 3% in a year? That is all Harriet would get. However, suppose the fund earned 10% the following year? Harriet would get her 5% based on a larger fund amount. As the fund grew in value so would the amount Harriet would receive as it would be 5% of a bigger pie.

There are two other possible ideas. The attorney could write the agreement so that there was a catch-up option. The lean year of 3% could have a make-up provision. Again, there are tax consequences, and a little more administrative complexity.

There is another possible item that could be included. Harriet had a son named Terry, and she wanted her son to have some inheritance. No problem. The CRUT could be set up to pay out to Harriet until she died, and it then would pay out to her son Terry for up to twenty years AFTER Harriet's death. Now, such an arrangement would reduce the value of the charitable gift and the charitable deduction, but that may not have been so important to Harriet. Of course, she could reduce Terry's pay out period to ten years. That would increase the charitable deduction amount.

Donors and advancement officers need to understand irrevocability. In setting up a CRUT, the commitment to charity is irrevocable. The donor cannot enjoy the tax treatment and then want the asset back. So, these are serious matters for everyone concerned. A second aspect is that while the commitment to charity is irrevocable, the donor can set these up so that the recipient charity might be revoked and a new one selected. Let's give an example.

Suppose there is a $1 million CRUT and there are two qualified charities who would each get 50% of the remainder interest on the death of the donor. The CRUT could be set up such that the donor could revoke the remainder interest for one or both charities. If they did that, the trust agreement would have to be modified to name a new recipient or two. A donor might want to do something like that if they thought the charity was going bad. Each of the new entities would have to be, of course, qualified charities. Most large charities have an in-house attorney or a network of qualified attorneys, to draw up such the agreements. If donors named several charities, that is fine. Of course, if the charity went through the time and effort to draw up the agreement, they likely would expect to be irrevocably a recipient. Maybe not 100%, but enough of the remainder that it is worth it for them to pay the attorney. Many charities will draw up the CRUT at no expense to the donor for that reason. They would not want to have their remainder interest revoked, and they would draw it up that way.

Let's recap. With the CRUT donors can: by-pass capital gains tax on appreciated assets; receive a charitable tax deduction; experience no capital gains tax on assets growing in the trust; reduce possible estate tax; and receive income for life that could keep pace with inflation. If Harriet had a husband, it could be set up for a two life pay out that would cover her and her husband. Further, they could add their son Terry for a set term if they chose. It is a powerful device, and for some people it solves a lot of problems. It is a boon for the charity.

Charitable Gift Annuity for Home

Another way to plan a charitable gift is give a home to a charity in a simple trust agreement that allows the owners to live in their home as long as they live. They maintain the home and pay taxes and insurance. In exchange, the charity agrees to pay the donors a fixed annuity to the husband and wife for both of their lives. They would obtain a charitable deduction that can be carried over for a least five years. Upon the death of both the husband and the wife, the charity owns the property. The home is not part of the estate tax consideration.

For some people this is a great component for their overall tax planning. In California, many people stay in their home for a long time as a means of controlling their property taxes. Their home is often their largest asset. They have social security and perhaps their pension or an Individual Retirement Account (IRA). But as time goes on, they could use some extra cash each month. Their home is a great asset but they don't want to sell it. This type of gift allows their home to generate income.

The charity must make sure that it is worth it on their side. If the couple is young, a lot can happen to housing prices in the next, say, twenty years. Suppose the owner and the charity agree the value of the house is $1 million, but years later when they sell it, the home only brings in $750,000. In the meantime, they will have paid out annuities based on that much higher figure. The charity also must do its due diligence to make sure there are no environmental hazards, and the house does not require a lot of work for resale. Because of advances in science and medicine, environmental considerations have become an important consideration. The presence of mold, lead, radon, and asbestos, are examples of more recent problems for which non-profits need to look. Still, the house for annuity can be a great option for a donor, and another way that a charity can receive a gift.

Banks and qualified financial institutions have their own version of this called the reverse mortgage. It is similar, but instead of a charity getting the remaining interest, the bank does. The fees should be examined as well as the payout. The chief difference is that with the non-profit tax-exempt recipient, the donor receives a charitable tax deduction. In addition, the donor gets the satisfaction of helping their favorite cause. Banks generally are not a favorite cause.

Charitable Lead Trust (CLT)

There is one more type of trust that may be worth mentioning. It is a little trickier, and there are several variations, but for some people it may be valuable. Suppose Paul has a large net worth and a good income. He wants to help a charity; but he is also concerned about the future of his son, James. He can set up a CLT such that the charity receives income from his gift of stock, or some income generating asset, for a set period. Say ten years. In this case, the charity will receive the income earned for the ten years. Paul does not pay income tax on the earnings. This is very helpful to the charity and Paul receives tax relief. Paul loses the income, but he doesn't care. He gets a tax deduction for his gift. At the end of Pauls's life, or ten years, the assets go to James.

It could also be the case that Paul has the asset revert to himself as a hedge against an uncertain future when he may need the income. Some of the variations concern who is owner of the trust, and that has implications for both the donor and the charity. This requires some sophisticated tax planning by professionals.

INSURANCE

Insurance may have an important role in the estate plans of a person. We have already discussed the idea that if a family farm or some such business has an owner that passes, the heirs may have a large estate tax obligation. But there are other uses too. One important feature of life insurance is that the beneficiary is not taxed for income. If a husband takes out a $1,000,000 policy and his wife is the beneficiary, upon the death of the husband, the wife receives the $1,000,000 tax free regardless of the size of the total estate. That is why in so many television murder mysteries, police detectives always look at the spouse. There is motive. Laying aside that rather macabre scenario, life insurance is generally a good thing for people who are married with children. An untimely death can impoverish a family.

There are celebrated cases of non-profits seeking to raise large amounts of money through life insurance. I generally run from anyone proposing these strategies. The scheme might work this way. The person taking out the policy would name the non-profit, usually a university, as either the owner or the beneficiary. Upon the death of the insured, the university would get 100% of the face value. Sometimes, the obliging insurance agent will set it up with a one-time premium. The full amount of the premium would be a gift to the university if it is paid by the donor and the university is the owner and beneficiary. The donor gets a charitable deduction. Of course, the agent gets paid a commission by the insurance company. As described, all is well. But these schemes can get tricky. Suppose the university agreed to pay multiple premiums until the insured died? There are so many variations on this use of insurance, and so many mixed motives, I do not recommend using life insurance this way. A donor should not confuse the charitable impulse. The insurance salesman has a different motive.

THE CRUMMEY TRUST

Having described the above abuses of a perfectly sound financial hedge against a life-ending catastrophe, there are very sound uses of life insurance in someone's estate plan. A person might, for instance, set up a trust with the unlikely name of a Crummey trust. The name derives from a 1968 case brought by *Crummey v. Commissioner of the Internal Revenue Service*. Thus, as of 2017 a person could contribute each year up to $14,000 for each beneficiary and invest the money in an insurance policy. This annual gift can be excluded from the estate and the resultant face value of the policy can be excluded from the previously mentioned $5.45 million estate tax exclusion. There are certain restrictions and notifications to the beneficiaries for each gift to the trust are required. Beneficiaries have the right to withdraw the gift, or insurance premium payment within a fixed period. Nonetheless, as the total value of the policy increases, all the proceeds upon the death of the insured goes to the beneficiaries. Unless, a person has a net worth above the current amount of $5.45 million, he doesn't need to concern himself with a Crummey Trust. One thing to keep in mind before discarding the idea is that a donor's estate may double or triple from the present. Well, it could also shrink! Insurance set up in a Crummey Trust might allow a great charitable dimension to a carefully planned estate.

MIX OF ALL THE ABOVE

I have been to enough planned giving seminars to know that highly qualified estate planning and planned giving attorneys can use a mix of all the above. The boxes and arrows can become quite complex. A qualified attorney can put together a plan that can increase the value of the estate for the heirs and increase the gifts to charity. This seemingly miraculous development occurs through bypassing capital gains taxes, using the charitable deduction, allowing the growth of the assets over time in a charitable trust that avoids capital gains taxes, and reducing the estate tax. As mentioned before, the only loser to a good estate plan will be the federal government. If a donor is a high net worth individual, or if an advancement officer works for a charity that has such supporters, it is very wise to learn about the serious advantages of the different types of planned gifts.

CHAPTER VI

Junk

POLITICAL DIRECT MAIL

NATURALLY IT IS NOT CALLED JUNK MAIL by those in that business. Direct marketing is the preferred term of art. Whatever it is called, when it is election season, and the season these days is increasingly long, when I go to the mail box it is filled with requests for money from political candidates and political causes. Direct mail, another term of art, is a way to raise funds for candidate campaigns or for a Political Action Committee (PAC). Why should a donor respond to a letter requesting money for a candidate running for office? A citizen surely does not have to make a gift of money. The dollar amounts requested are for much less than for the more elite political fundraiser in some home of a person of significant wealth.

That letter in that mail box is the result of a process that began when the recipient subscribed to a publication; made a gift to another candidate of the same party; or perhaps donated to a think tank that specializes in certain issue areas. These political fundraising letters position the candidate on the side of the angels and the opponent as a tool of the devil who will destroy the country. The gift that the recipient of the letter makes will make it possible for good to triumph over evil. Failure to give will allow evil to triumph over good. The standard letters are about six pages long and the candidate, or some widely recognized political leader, sign them. There are many exclamation points.

The candidate's campaign will have rented the name and address for a one-time use from another candidate, a publication, a political party, or an issue oriented cause. Some lists are more expensive than others based on previous results. Usually a campaign will test a small random selection of names from a much larger list. The standard test list is 5,000 names and addresses. If mailing to that select list comes close to breaking even, they will do it again with a bigger sample. If the campaign does not come close to breaking even, they will stop mailing to that list.

Speaking of breaking even, it is the DMA that keeps postage for bulk mailing low. If those who use direct mail had to use first class postage rates, there would be much less bulk mailings. The DMA used to stand for Direct Marketing Association, but it now stands for Data & Marketing Association. As you can imagine, it is a quite powerful lobby in Washington, DC, a city where they have many friends who use direct mail to get elected. Examine all your mail sometimes and you can see the range of categories. Aside from letters for candidates and causes there are the catalogues. Yes, the world is going digital, and snail mail may go the way of the milkman. (For those of you too young, milkmen used to deliver milk and other dairy products to porches.) We are not there yet.

In any case, political campaigns will retain a direct mail fundraising firm to run that part of the fundraising for them, and the firm gets paid for every letter mailed. There are well-known firms in the trade that specialize in political fundraising. Not only do they test lists, they test signatories, specific issues, envelope design, surveys, and just about everything. The reply envelopes and checks go to what is called a "caging company" that has special machines and procedures for opening the letters, recording the replies, and quickly depositing the money in the campaign's bank account. Sometimes the banks run the caging operation in their backroom. If the direct mail company is successful, the campaign might break even on a response rate of 2% for a given list and depending on the average gift. That means 98% of the recipients do not donate. There should be regular reports each month, or more, that are highly detailed on each list tested with the cost per letter mailed, the total amount raised from that list, the average gift level, and other such data. If a tested selected list comes close to break even, then immediately another mailing with a larger roll out is in order.

What good is breaking even? If the campaign has the names and addresses of people who sent money once, the campaign likely will realize a profit on the next mailing to these proven givers. The campaign may have located donors who will support the candidate repeatedly. A successful response rate on these so-called "house mailings" might be 7-10%. If this dynamic is going well just before an election, these letters keep the supporters informed and motivated and this, in turn, will motivate them to vote on election day. The campaign will keep mailing to a respondent until it is clear they will never get another gift again. If the respondent gives a larger amount, the campaign will keep that donor on their active house list longer. They likely will be invited to special events. It may not make much sense to send to people whose highest gift is $5 in the last two years, but it may make sense to mail to donors who gave at least $10 or more.

The campaign would have agreed beforehand with the direct mail company as to who owns the names and addresses of those who responded to a prospect mailing. If ownership is shared, the direct mail company will charge the campaign less. In that case, the direct mail company has the right to rent the names to others. When they rent, they declare the dates of a list that worked and the average gift, etc. Who wants to rent a stale list that doesn't work?

The accumulated house list needs to be periodically checked to make sure there are no duplicate records. Data entry is never 100% perfect and if a letter in the last name or a digit in the zip code is off, then there may be a new donor record created for the same person. Whoever is using the list needs to look for duplicates by running a "de-duper" program that checks by last names and zip codes. They can be quite sophisticated in looking for similar records that almost match. As you might imagine the possibility of duplicate donor records is ever present after each mailing. Sending several letters to the same person with errors in their name wastes money and angers recipients.

Once the fundraiser for the campaign, or the cause, turns over much of the direct mail fundraising program to an outside vender, how do they know that the letters are going out for their mailings or to the others to whom they rent the list? How do they know the vender isn't renting the list without paying the campaign or the organization who owns the names? The best way is to make sure the person in charge of fundraising for the candidate, or the non-profit, has their name, or a made-up name with their address, on the rental list. They can just add it in. Or, they could give the $25 dollars to make sure they are on the list. The vender does the same thing to protect his list from dishonest persons in the business. When the fundraiser or the direct mail company receive a mailing that is un-authorized, whoever is responsible for fundraising or legal enforcement needs to contact the company. That is a big no-no in the business, and whoever is caught will not have a business after that. A reputation for deceit travels very quickly. Well, mistakes do happen too, but the person in charge needs to mind the store.

If donors have a passion for one issue above all others, they often will contribute to a think tank, publication, or association that advocates issues they favor. In turn that association might rent their names to candidates that support their issue. The most powerful associations in the country usually have both an educational wing, where tax-deductions are allowed, and a political wing, where donations are not tax-deductible. The direct mail company will most certainly have suggestions for candidates as to which publications or which donor lists might work, especially if they own or have the right to use a given list. A candidate may wish to test a list from another candidate who shares their passion and who has high name recognition. The direct mail company must exercise control over mailing dates and usage lest a donor be deluged on the same day by too many candidates or causes.

Direct mail fundraising for candidates is sometimes unpredictable in another way. For example, in more rural areas, Democrats are often Second Amendment enthusiasts. Hypothetically, mailing to the National Rifle Association (NRA) list, generally more Republican than not, might work for a pro Second Amendment Democrat. The NRA cares less about Republican or Democrat labels. If a candidate's campaign is based on the issue of global warming, it might choose to test a donor list from Greenpeace or the Environmental Defense Fund.

Despite the growth of social media in the last decade, political direct mail will be here for some time to come.

Non-Profit Direct Mail

Perhaps a donor is not a very political person. Nonetheless, if they have a pulse and are over 25, they likely have gotten a letter in the mail asking for support for some cause or another. Non-profits often have a direct mail program as one component of their efforts to raise money. Many of the same practices apply that work for a political candidate. It is a technique to raise money for the non-profit cause. Non-profits should at least consider whether direct mail is a viable option as a part of their advancement effort.

I recall the first time I received such a direct mail letter. With a "Dear Mr. Warder" I was invited to join a seemingly prestigious Board with a list of seemingly very important people. I had been personally selected "after careful review" as I recall. There were some annual meetings I would be allowed to attend with these important people who supported a cause about which I was concerned. However, before that I had to give to the organization a significant gift. It was from a non-profit tax-exempt organization in Washington, DC that did public policy research. I threw it away after looking at the offer a little more carefully, and reflecting further on my meager resources. Organizations run these types of fundraising tactics whether it is to save the planet, help a local program for the poor, help a far-away program for the poor, fight cancer, save children, help abandoned animals, or help deserving students at alma mater.

I will confess that in due course I have run direct mail programs for a non-profit. If such an organization is thinking about testing such a program, there are certain things that need to be considered. The first thing would be to ensure that the program does not harm the reputation of the organization. Direct mail programs work on the emotions of the prospective donor sometimes in very crude ways. While the letter may return well for many, excuse me, low dollar donors, it may in the longer run work against the reputation of the organization you represent. If a given letter reflects well on the organization, it may not pull very well to justify such a program involving prospect and house mailings as described earlier.

The President or CDO should have final say on the letter content. It is a good practice to have an attorney look it over as well. I recall numerous instances where an in-house writer for the non-profit would create letters that everyone up and down the chain of command loved. We would test it, and it did very poorly. Then a copy writer for the direct mail company would write a letter that seemed rather like a cartoon, and it pulled very well. As is true for many things, you never really know what works until you test it.

I have located wealthy donors who have sent in large gifts through these mailings. It's a great thing, but it really screws up the statistics for a list. Suppose a respondent gives $10,000 and no one else on the random list of 5,000 gives a penny. The average gift for that list is $2. So, you must look at all kinds of averages to conclude if it makes sense to roll out a larger sample. Finding that one donor that gives $10,000 is very rare, but it does happen. Such a donor should be taken off the direct mail list and be treated very differently by the organization. A donor of that magnitude thereafter will never be on any rental list. Likely that person will be a great donor over the years.

Unless a non-profit is very large, I would advise that most not try to do direct mail in-house. It is highly complex and detailed. Reputable direct mail companies know what they are doing and have resources and expertise. Since they get paid per letter mailed, they are usually optimistic. So, prospect mailing and house mailings need careful monitoring to make sure they are working. With the advent of email and social media, direct mail may be a dying industry. Nonetheless, when I go these days to the mail box, it is still filled with mass mailings. Fortunately, as I walk back to my living room, I pass the garbage can.

If a non-profit has a very large house list of donors, it has the possibility of renting portions of the house list. It could be a valuable source of additional revenue. No one rents names of their high dollar donors. If a non-profit does wish to gain some revenue from renting their house file list, it should be noted that donors might migrate from their organization to another. Well, migration may work both ways.

Digital Giving

While direct mail came to be quite popular for some charities and political causes in the 1970s, more recently similar principles have been adapted to the digital age. Those in the field of advancement need to pay attention to this rapidly changing method of raising funds. Knowledge of digital media is spreading. When a person opens his inbox on his computer or smartphone, he often receives emails that ask him to give to a cause or to buy something. (Occasionally there is that email from Nigeria informing the lucky recipient that he has a very large amount of money and they need to provide their bank number to receive it.) Sending blast emails cost the sender very little per email sent. It avoids the expense of postage as well as the expense of printing, folding, and stuffing the letter into the envelope. The method eliminates caging expense to open the envelope, record the gift, and deposit it in the bank. A person can make the gift from his credit card, PayPal, or some such service. Of course, there are programs for smart phones and computers to send most of these email solicitations into the trash. The recipient can block specific senders. Still, crafty candidates or causes may seek counter measures to thwart whatever screening a recipient sets up. It is also true that sometimes organizations simply use the email route for invitations to an event.

Most candidates and non-profit organizations have a website that directs a donor to a link to make a gift. Every cause should have this option. If a person takes the time to go to a website, that is more than half of the battle. Whatever money is spent for website design to make it attractive and easy, that is money well spent. It is also a place where the cause can provide all the information that was discussed earlier such as the main programs, noteworthy achievements, news, leadership, Board of Directors, 990 form, and all the rest. Many political campaigns and non-profits have mastered this "click and give" technology very well. If a person goes to a website and cannot find much information about the programs, coming events, or achievements, and if the financial information is murky, these are all red flags. The advancement officer needs to make the case to his organization to have a website that is attractive, informative, and simple to use for a potential donor. It is increasingly important. The activity on each page of the website is also an excellent way to see which parts of your organization are attractive by counting which pages have the most traffic. Someone in the advancement office needs to be monitoring the support that comes in and what may prompt it.

Increasingly all our digital activity is accessible by many different entities. Credit cards, Internet service providers for telephone, television, and movies, Google, Facebook, Instagram, Snapchat, GPS tracking of smart phones, and the FastTrak device in cars all provide information about a person's digital profile. Who has access to this information? How can they use it to sell you something or to elicit a donation to a cause through an advertisement on social media? What are the details in those contracts that pop-up on our computers and smart phones that end in "I accept?" These are all questions that people and their governments will be answering in the years ahead. No doubt the answers will impact the solicitation of gifts by non-profits and political campaigns in the future.

The Telephone

It is dinner time and Ed and Linda Smith have just sat down to dinner. The telephone rings. Ed picks up the phone to answer and there is silence for just a moment until a voice comes on. More than likely it is a robot calling. Alternatively, it might be a person waiting for the software to kick in to connect the live caller to Ed. These days many residential phones have caller identification or recording devices that allow a person to listen to the recording or the pitch without picking up. It's a good buffer.

In any case, if Ed answers the telephone and there is a person or recording telling him that he has been "specially selected," or he has won a free trip to somewhere, or it's the local police benevolent society, or the Internal Revenue Service, or any number of things, he should hang up. If he wishes to be polite and it seems the call is from a human being, he could say "thank you, but I am not interested." The reason is simple. Ed has no idea with whom he is speaking. Charities should not cold-call prospects. It can harm their reputation.

Increasingly all manner of companies and organizations have access to both your residential and smartphone numbers. No one should ever agree to use his credit card number to make a gift to an unknown phone caller who makes a solicitation. If a would-be donor initiates the phone call to a known charity to a known person, a credit card gift may be acceptable. It's much simpler than writing a check and the donor may get credit for rewards.

In the past, phone calls were so personal. Not these days. Still, a call could be from a legitimate source trying to inform the resident that his water will be turned off for two hours the next day between 2 pm and 4 pm. It could be the pharmacy calling to say a prescription is ready. So, it is wise for phone call recipients to answer, or, later, to listen to the recording of the call.

I will admit that I have called people using lists through an automated call program. It was to get people out to vote for a certain candidate. It's not easy work. So, I do have some sympathy for the person making the calls. Nonetheless, a prospect should not divulge information or make a gift from an unsolicited phone call.

One exception would be a phone call to a donor as a follow-up to an invitation to attend an event sponsored by the charity. If the donor is important to the organization, the advancement officer should make the call to a donor where there is a relationship. One time I did try to implement a program where a phone call follow-up was made by trained callers to a house list of direct mail donors. It was complex and not worth it.

The telephone is a very personal instrument. Non-profits should not harm their brand by abusing this most personal means of communication. If some non-profit proves me wrong by results they achieve over time, I yield to the technique as practiced.

CHAPTER VII

Who is Asking?

"He's a man way out there in the blue riding
on a smile and a shoeshine. And when they
start not smiling back—that's an earthquake...
A salesman is got to dream boy."
—Charley, *Death of a Salesman*

THE ADVANCEMENT OFFICER

EACH CHARITABLE ORGANIZATION HAS PEOPLE, sometimes many people, who solicit people for gifts. If the organization has only a few employees, likely it will be the President. Some charities have hundreds of employees and scores of people who ask donors for support. They are frequently referred to as advancement officers, development officers, solicitors, or simply fundraisers. Personally, I never liked being called a fundraiser. Of course, the bottom line is that the job is to raise funds. The non-profit pays a person to do that job. Fair enough. Nonetheless, let me explain further the reason "fundraiser" is a poor job title.

Whenever a solicitor asks a person for a donation, they do so on behalf of the organization. It really is an attempt to make an agreement, a kind of contract if you will, between the donor and the group. Indeed, for large gifts it may very well be a formal contract. The organization has the obligation to deliver, and the solicitor represents that it will do so. If there was success in getting the donation, and the group did not deliver the service, the solicitor has failed in his obligation to the donor. In a large organization, there are many titles. If you are asking someone for money on behalf of the organization, you are, even at the most junior position, an advancement officer. You are not simply a fundraiser. The matter should be taken seriously by the person who asks and by the organization who sends them out.

It takes all kinds of people to make a fundraising team. There are people who maintain records of gifts and the record of the relationship with the donor. Someone with computer software skills selects who will be invited to a reception or dinner. There are people who manage events. Someone writes the copy for the dinner program and someone designs it. Someone must take pictures at the event for the publication that goes out to the donors. If it a college, then someone is responsible for alumni relations. Media and public relations play a role as does marketing. The larger the organization, the greater the complexity. It is somewhat like an army. There are a whole variety of specialties in the army ranging from mechanics, to purchasing agents, to cooks, etc. But, finally, in an army there is the rifleman who pulls the trigger. In a sense, the advancement officer is the trigger puller of the advancement division. The team works to get them in front of the right person at the right time to take their best shot. The advancement officer makes the ask to obtain the best gift possible from the donor.

Regardless of the type of personality solicitors have, when they walk into that prospect's office or meet them at a restaurant, donors should have a warm feeling in their heart. If they don't have that feeling, solicitors need to bring something to gladden the hearts of prospects whether it be a smile, a compliment, or some signal that they are looking forward to the visit with a person that is both respected and liked. You do not want to hear or sense: "Uh-oh, here comes Mike. Better keep your hand on your wallet." I have heard that line on more than one occasion, and I always smile at the joke. It's usually said in a small group of potential or current donors. Well, being an advancement officer isn't quite like what Charley said in the above quote about Willy Loman in Arthur Miller's *Death of a Salesman*, but there is an element of truth to it. It should not be that prospects are dreading a meeting with advancement officers. But wait a moment, how is it that the solicitor finds himself in front of that prospect? We will be exploring that in the pages ahead, but we need first to discuss the language of money.

Language of Money

Suppose there is a thirty-year old young man, David, who is renting an apartment; has a student loan that is not yet paid; has some credit card debt; leases his car; and has no spouse or children. He studied communications in a good private college a few years back. He is an advancement officer for a charity and he has an appointment with a couple, Jim and Alice, who are about seventy years old and who live in a nice home; have a net worth of about $10 million in their business, home, and a combination of traditional IRAs, Roth IRAs, and stocks that have appreciated over time. Jim and Alice, married now for forty-five years, built a successful real estate business selling homes and then apartments. That business is also part of their net worth. The husband had served in the Vietnam War. They started with little money and have three successful children who are happily married, and they have between them nine grandchildren. One of their children works at the office with them, and is being groomed to lead the business when Jim and Alice can no longer do so. What is the possibility of this young advancement officer to solicit successfully a major gift for them?

Unless David has a sense of what this couple went through and what issues, both financial and personal, they currently face, it will be tough going no matter if he has a winning smile, polished shoes, and determination. The gap is just too large. The couple were each born as World War II ended. Their parents went through the Great Depression and then World War II. David was born as the Cold War was ending. He doesn't have much sense of the history these possible donors and their families lived through. History isn't a big issue on most social media.

But let's assume that David knew something of what this couple and their family went through to bring them where they are today.

He was a good listener. He learned Jim and Alice had saved their real estate commissions to start their business. He knew their marriage had its ups and downs but their faith and their commitment to each other kept them together. David was a good listener and he learned something of their life story. He was phenomenal in that sense. Jim and Alice liked the young man.

Having a sense of the history this couple went through was not David's problem. His problem was that he did not know the difference between a traditional Individual Retirement Account (IRA) and a Roth IRA; the difference between long and short-term capital gains taxes, the relative merits of Charitable Remainder Uni-Trusts compared to Charitable Gift Annuities; the tax consequences of growth stocks and value stocks; how a Living Trust differs from a Will that goes through probate (whatever that is); or term life insurance in contrast to whole life insurance.

I mention this rather dramatic illustration to show that being a good listener and having some element of charm can only get an advancement officer so far in the effort to solicit a large gift from a couple that is well-qualified to give one. There is no substitute to knowing something of the world of money. It tells the donor you are a serious person. For those who are just starting out, I suggest several books that I found to be of use. In addition to making a person a better advancement officer, these will help anyone develop their own financial plans.

One of my all-time favorite books is *The Only Investment Book You Will Ever Need* written by Andrew Tobias, a financial journalist. It was first published in 1978 and has gone through so many new editions that I hesitate to write a number. It is witty and mercifully short. He gives an overview of the different kinds of investments. Every so often I would give new editions to our children, the last being the 2010 edition shortly after the collapse of 2008. One idea is not to spend more money than you earn. It's quaint, I know.

Another investment book, a bit more scholarly but still accessible, is *A Random Walk Down Wall Street* by Burton G. Malkiel, a Princeton economist. It too has had many, many editions. It was first published in 1973, and the edition I have is 2015. I had heard about the book and something of the theory for years, but I bought it, and it reinforced my thinking. So, of course, I recommend it. The thesis can be stated various ways. I would put it this way. Experts really do not know which stocks are going up or down. In general, the stock market does go up over time, so a person would be well served to invest regularly over time in a diversified group of stocks.

Anything by John Bogle, the Founder of Vanguard Mutual Funds, is good. One book is *The Little Book of Common Sense Investing*. Jack always makes the same point since he was a student at Princeton. He started index investing. The idea is to buy a large basket of stocks, an index, like the Total Stock Market Fund. It includes big companies and small; old companies and new; and high tech and mining. Buy the whole market. In a given year a particular stock may do well. The nearly impossible trick is to know which year and to make the right choices ahead of everyone else who buys and sells stocks. In a given year an actively managed mutual fund that tries to pick winners and losers may do well. Again, the problem is knowing when the fund is going up and when it is going down relative to the market or its niche. Over time, it is very hard to beat broad indexes. Further, the indexes have low costs and are tax efficient. These two factors make a big difference over time. What about bonds? The same thing. Buy an index that has long term bonds and short term bonds, as well as safe and junk (high yield and high risk) bonds. Vanguard has a Total Bond Fund. It keeps expenses low. Since there is little turnover, it is very good at keeping taxes low. As Jack points out, commissions and taxes take much of the fun out of investing and really are a drag on building that nest egg. I call him Jack because I met him once. Good guy and a legend.

Lastly, you might read Peter Lynch. He takes a different approach. One of his books is called *Beating the Street*. Peter had one of the most successful stock picking stints ever when he managed the Magellan Fund, one of the Fidelity Mutual Funds. Peter explains his thoughts on how to pick a stock that is under-valued so that the buyer can enjoy the ride up as its stock price soars, and then know when to sell it before it tanks. Sure, there are capital gains, and sure there is a commission to pay the brokerage firm. But, if the stock picker picks well and has an acute sense of timing that is better than others, they can do very well. Stock picking is risky, and there are many smart people who have instant access to massive information. And it is especially tricky, I have found, knowing when to sell. If a person buys a stock that is doubling or tripling, why on earth would they sell it? Chances are they wouldn't since they are in love with this stock. Until it tanks. That is the worst time to sell.

Market timing is very difficult if not impossible over time, and so is timing the sale of a specific stock. There are very smart people at mutual funds or pension funds, with access to much information quicker than most. They will invest or sell shares of a stock worth hundreds of millions of dollars with a push of a button. They can move the price of a stock up or down. It is hard to compete with these folks. All the leaders of mutual funds and pension funds watch each other like hawks. They, like any of us, tend to jump on bandwagons. However smart, and however well-informed, no one wants to miss the next super stock or bull-market. If the other major fund stock pickers are going in a certain direction, better jump on board with them. The smaller investor is usually late to the party and pays a higher price for a stock.

If a person is starting out as an advancement officer to raise funds for a good cause from people of wealth, these four books will allow him to keep up the conversation. Even if they are young, they can have a bit of wisdom beyond their years. And, incidentally, this young professional might become better at managing whatever money they have earned and then saved. Donors to charities generally are not impressed with people who are not sensible with money.

WHO ARE THESE MILLIONAIRES?

Aside from knowing something of the language of money and investing, how did wealthy people, like Jim and Alice, become wealthy? Who are they? After all, if it was just a question of investing, why wouldn't every literate person who read the four books I mentioned become wealthy? Are there common characteristics shared among these people who have become millionaires?

In the 1990s, two men, Thomas Stanley and William Danko, wrote a book, *The Millionaire Next Door: The Surprising Secrets of America's Wealthy*. That young advancement officer mentioned earlier, may just wonder: how did that couple become wealthy? This little book, based on thousands of interviews, gives some insight. The two authors have kept at it, but that first book, now in many more editions, has the gist of the books that followed.

Stanley and Danko found that most wealthy people, not the movie stars, athletes, or Wall Street sharks, save money all along. They don't spend more than they take in. They are not extravagant. They also stay married. Divorce is very expensive among other things. They often will pick a profession that is not glamorous, but necessary. I always like to mention garbage collection and landfill management. OK. That is an extreme case. I once mentioned this example to a student and, oddly enough, his parents were in the business. He was excited to tell me that people pay his family to take their commodities. It is like getting something valuable for free. Then they sorted all that is in garbage and resell that which has the most value. He was quite excited by the garbage business. Or, as he called it, the commodities business.

One very odd trait was that these average millionaires will often tend to buy cars according to weight and price. Rather than buying an international exotic car every other year, they often will buy a Ford 150 pick-up truck or a sedan and hang on to it for a good number of years. Literally, they get more car poundage per dollar than most. They don't buy watches that are very expensive pieces of jewelry that don't work very well. They buy clothes off the rack.

We have far too many attorneys out of work because wealthy parents often love their children to become lawyers. It is a respectable profession. They have heard that attorneys do very well, and they have paid attorneys some good money over the years. So, many wealthy parents will send their children to study law only to find there are many, many outstanding lawyers already. Google it. What about starting a roofing business? Every house needs a roof, and after a while, it is going to leak during that big rain. Eventually it will need to be replaced. Or maybe run a junk yard and sell spare parts. There, of course, is plumbing. Not glamourous, but oh so necessary. Then too, all big buildings need janitorial services. What child growing up wants to be in the business of garbage, roofing, junk, plumbing, or office cleaning? The point is, there is not much competition. These millionaires that Stanley and Danko describe work hard at their business and improve it every year. They don't do drugs and they are not alcoholics.

They do not move much either. They buy a good house and stay in it for a long time, and thereby avoid real estate commissions and continually fixing up the new house. They usually buy a house in a decent neighborhood, but not posh. Their children go to better public schools, and they know that they are going to have to earn their way in this world. They do not believe they are magically entitled to wealth. They often go to state universities.

I would suggest that every advancement officer read this book, or one like it. They will have a better idea in many instances about the people with whom they are speaking.

PERSONALITY

While there are many different facets to a large charity, and they should all work together, let's dig a little deeper about the people whose job is to ask people for money in personal meetings. There is no one type of person best suited for this, but it is important to be interested in people. Whether talking to a billionaire or a person who might make a smaller gift, a good advancement officer needs to be the type of person who is curious about what makes that person get up in the morning. What makes them tick? What do they like? What don't they like? How did they get to the position they are now? More crudely, how did they make their money? Who are their peers or friends? Are they happily married? Do they have children? How are their children doing? Generally, what is the situation they are in? Are there little clues dropped in conversation about their deeper concerns? What is it in the cause that the solicitor represents that would appeal the most to that potential donor?

If an advancement officer is not interested in people or comfortable with people, chances are they may not have what is required to be an advancement officer. Like any human endeavor, it takes all kinds to raise money. Some people are excellent at one-on-one communication. Others are not, but they have strong analytical skills. Some people are methodical, while others are intuitive. Donors come with all different types of personalities too, and one advancement officer may do better with one prospect than another. Solicitors, whether a woman or a man, come in all shapes and sizes as do donors. The solicitor must also have good judgment. Asking for the right gift at the wrong time is bad. Asking for a gift prematurely may sour the donor on the organization. Patience and determination are valuable traits to cultivate in a person who seeks gifts. An ability to take rejection well is invaluable.

If a solicitor is going to ask someone for a gift, it is a psychological necessity that they believe in the organization they represent. The advancement officer should be a donor to the cause, even if it a small amount. It is very hard to ask someone to give to a charity if the person asking hasn't given something. A young solicitor with student loans, car payments, rent, etc. may say they cannot afford it. If they can afford that Starbucks coffee once a day and a recent version of a smart phone, they could afford a modest gift. Some people are just not cut out to ask other people for money to support the organization. There is no shame in that.

Prospect Research

It is a rare advancement officer who can understand a seventy-year-old billionaire. That billionaire is not going to spill his guts to an advancement officer. He will want to speak to the CEO, the person in charge, or a senior executive. Fortunately, there is research that can help an advancement officer bridge the gap and facilitate a path toward a gift and a meeting with the CEO. A meeting between these two for soliciting a seven-figure gift is going to come at the end of a lengthy process of research and trust building. That advancement officer and the CEO of the non-profit should know as much about that person as is humanly possible. In the era of the Internet, it has become a little easier. Aside from search engines, there is all manner of information about property owned, Security and Exchange Commission reporting related to stock buys and sells, ownership, marital status, number of children, past positions held, legal proceedings against, gifts to charitable organizations; board positions held, college and graduate degrees; criminal convictions, and much else. Usually a large charity will hire a company that can provide some of this information and update it periodically and automatically for names the charity has on its data base. They will rank prospects by estimated net worth. Frankly, most people would be surprised at how much these companies can discover. Of course, they are not infallible. It is also true that some people are careful about hiding their wealth through trusts and other mechanisms. These information resources help to put the solicitor in the ballpark, but still there are many unknowns.

The worst thing is to ask for a gift during an introductory meeting. Rather, a solicitor would want to let the potential donor know that he shares their passion for the issues the group supports; that it has some outstanding people of consequence working for the cause; and that it is making a difference. He might point to mentions in the press; television appearances; references and endorsements from people of consequence. I am not saying to turn down a gift, but in the long run, it is important to get to know what that donor really cares about. Perhaps there is something, or there could be something, that the organization does that would speak to a donor's deeper concerns.

Charities use all the methods mentioned above: letters, phone calls, social media, visits, and such. The larger charities have an array of engagement mechanisms. A potential donor might have an interest in speaker events, conferences, recognition dinners, trips, golf tournaments, and other such things. As the relationship moves along and some early gifts are made, the donor might be asked to join an Advisory Board of some kind. The last thing along this path of increasing engagement might be an offer to join the Board of Directors. Some donors do not want to be bothered with board memberships, and would prefer to remain low-key.

Frequently advancement officers will join Rotary, Kiwanis, and other services clubs so they will meet and get to know new potential donors. The organization will often pay the dues. The more senior an advancement officer is, the more exclusive are the clubs. Advancement officers need to get out of the office and meet people. Attending internal meetings are necessary, but they all serve the purpose of getting the solicitor in front of a potential donor.

A Word on Religion

As an advancement officer does his research on a given potential donor, he would be well served to understand their religious orientation. Obviously if they are Hindu, Buddhist, Moslem, or Jewish, quoting a verse from the New Testament may not be helpful to say the least. It would show the donor that you have no idea with whom you are speaking. Even a Protestant or Catholic likely would be put off by somehow using Scripture for eliciting a gift. Further, within the Christian faith there are many denominations with some focused on the Bible while others are charismatic. To others liturgy and the sacraments are of greater importance. Some potential donors are agnostic or atheistic.

The gift officer should know with whom they are dealing. In this

rapidly shrinking world, increasingly advancement officers are dealing with people of all different faiths and cultures. I have encountered
some Americans who sincerely believe that non-Christians are not
going to be donors. That just exhibits their ignorance or prejudice. All
the major religions of the world encourage charity. It is wise to study
at least a bit about the religious beliefs of a potential donor if only to
avoid offense. Nor would I write off an atheist for a cause, but it does
depend on the cause. Perhaps they are a believer in free enterprise, and
if that is the cause, the door is open.

A few examples of the teachings about charity from some different religions might further drive the point home. What follows is not
meant to be an authoritative explanation of the nuanced differences
of the concept of charity in some of the major religions. It is to make
the point that all the major religions recognize an ethical obligation to
help others less fortunate.

In the Christian Bible, the *Book of Proverbs* 11:24-25 (New International Version) states: "One person gives freely, yet gains even more;
another withholds unduly, but comes to poverty. A generous person
will prosper; whoever refreshes others will be refreshed."

To the Jew the *Book of Proverbs*, part of what Christians call the *Old
Testament*, is part of the *Tanakh*. The *Tanakh* and the *Old Testament*
are virtually identical, though the order of the books and some of the
numbering of verses is different (And there are well-founded reasons
why this is so.). From a widely cited 11th century commentary on the
Tanakh, called the *Midrash Mishle*, there is the quote: "If you see a man
giving liberally, it means his wealth will grow; if you see one who shuns
charity, it means his wealth will dwindle."

What about Islam? There are the Five Pillars of Islam. These are
the keys to a Moslem's view of salvation. The 3rd pillar is *Zakat*, which
roughly translates as paying an alms tax to benefit those in need. There
is variation in understanding of this teaching according to the different legal schools of Islam and according to particular countries where
Islam is the majority religion. In some countries it is voluntary, where-

as in others it is mandatory. Regardless, the idea is that by giving one's wealth to help the poor, a person purifies his soul.

In Hinduism there is a Sanskrit word, *dana*, that connotes the virtue of charity or the giving of alms. In the *Bhagavad Gita*, translated as the *Song of the Lord*, and referred to by some scholars as the summation of the Hindu religion, from Chapter 17, verse 20: "Giving simply because it is right to give, without thought of return, at a proper time, in proper circumstances, and to a worthy person is *sattvic* (pure, or without strings) giving."

In the Chinese philosophy of Confucianism, there is the concept of *ren*, roughly translated as benevolence or "loving men." It is mentioned in the *Analects*, the teachings of Confucius. In verse 6:30 a student asked Confucius "If there is someone who can give extensively to the people and relieve the multitudes, what do you think of him? Can he be called a man of humanity? The Master said: 'Far more than a man of humanity. He must be a sage.'"

The point to this overly simplistic reference to the concept of charity in different religions is that advancement officers should take it upon themselves to gain some familiarity of the person from whom they are seeking a donation. Religion and culture may differ, but there are some universals when it comes to the idea of making a gift to benefit others who need help. Charity is good.

PROSPECT ASSIGNMENTS

Within every organization, there is a person who assigns solicitors to donors. Without this, a donor might be asked by multiple people for meetings and then gifts. If the organization is long standing, often these relations have been determined over time. Suppose there are some highly successful senior advancement officers who have been working for an organization and they leave to work elsewhere or to retire. Who inherits the donors? Someone must decide. In a small organization it is the President. In a large organization, it is the Chief Development Officer (CDO), or a person with some such title.

Frankly, it is a difficult job. The CDO is responsible for all gift revenue. It is also true that CDOs are expected personally to solicit large gifts. Naturally this person has clout within the charity. Without gifts, not much is going to be happening to allow the organization to grow. Even in a college where students pay tuition, as well as room and board, those funds likely won't cover a new dormitory or scholarships that allow the college to compete for the best students. Nor will it cover a rise in the quality of the faculty. That will take additional gifts. There are thousands of colleges competing for the best students and faculty. In some charities that serve the homeless, abandoned animals, children with severe disabilities or illnesses, donations are even more central. The CDO's role is key in non-profits. While a donor may speak to a variety of people in an organization, there should be only one who asks for the donation. That is the prospect manager who manages the relation. The CDO assigns prospects.

Prospect assignment reminds me of a lesson I learned when I was the "new kid" who got on a truck at 5:00 am to pick oranges with veteran orange pickers in Southern California. It seemed simple enough. You have a bag and orange clippers and you go to work on the trees. Not so. Each picker was assigned a tree by the foreman. The veteran pickers, who were highly skilled, were assigned to small trees with big oranges. The newest member of the team, me, was assigned to the tallest trees with the smallest oranges. All orange pickers were paid 32 cents per crate. Believe me when I say that a novice working off a ladder on a tall tree with small oranges must spend much more time picking many more oranges before that crate fills up. Picking on the ground is so much easier than high up on a ladder. It is a little like the CDO assigning solicitors to prospective donors. Even as a young man, I had to admit, the pickers assigned to the small trees with big oranges were masters. They seemed to have multiple oranges in the air simultaneously going into their bag, while I dangled off of a ladder struggling to make sure one orange made it into the bag.

Another example. I was a caddy at a golf course as a teenager. When

I was brand new, the caddy master would assign me to the worst golfers who also did not tip well. The big tippers, who often were the better golfers, were assigned to the caddies who knew golf, could show deference to the golfer, and could give, when asked, competent advice about the right club to hit or insight into the break of a putt on the green. These caddies had experience. They made more money. A new caddy can learn a lot by listening to the veterans. Sometimes, a golfer would request the caddy master to assign a certain caddy whom he preferred.

Raising money is much more complicated, but the principle involved for assigning orange pickers or caddies is like assigning advancement officers to donor prospects. The CDO assigns people whom he thinks will do the best. It is in his interest to do so, if he is results oriented. The proven highly skilled advancement officers are assigned to the donors who have the greatest potential. Well, that is the theory. Those assignments are key.

The donor who gives the largest gifts may want to deal with the CEO. After all, this is the person who can guarantee the organization will follow through with any agreement between the donor and the organization. The donor may also feel he warrants such attention. Usually that type of meeting comes at the end of the cultivation process that involves prior meetings between the solicitor and the donor.

In assigning prospects, the general idea is to match like with like. Just as there is a hierarchy in the world of the donors, there is a hierarchy in the advancement officers. They are assigned titles related to their rank whether it be Executive Vice President (EVP) for Advancement, Senior VP, Associate VP, Assistant VP, etc. The titles reflect the institution's designation to help the donor know better with whom they are dealing. The titles may help. Still, if the functional equivalent of a private first class discovers and brings in a new prospect who is a billionaire, it is hard then to assign another person to this prospect. If it happens a second time, the organization needs to promote that advancement officer!

What do the donor and the solicitor have in common? The more they have in common the better. These assignment decisions are more art than science. For example, if a donor is a graduate of the University of California at Berkeley, and someone on the staff has a degree from the same university, that might help. If a potential donor is a devout Catholic, a solicitor who is a devout Catholic might work better than a secularist. If a potential donor is from West Virginia, and someone on the staff is from West Virginia, that might work. If a prospect is a sports fanatic, then it might be good to assign a sports fanatic. Finally, there is no substitute for a highly prepared, competent, and empathetic solicitor who can discern the motivations of a potential donor and who understands where in the organization that potential gift might best fit. Sometimes people just click.

It is also true that a new advancement officer should go out and find his own new prospects. Get out in the community. Attend events that may have like-minded people who may become prospects. Not so incidentally, a solicitor should always have an ample supply of business cards wherever they are. It may seem too obvious to mention. I know a highly successful real estate syndicator with a very large net worth. Wherever he goes, he always has a thick wad of business cards held together by a rubber band. He is not stingy with his cards, nor is he shy about asking anyone he meets for their business card. Even so, he uses these encounters to show interest and regard for the person he meets by giving a card. You never know.

If another solicitor has joined some downtown club, find a different club. Perhaps a solicitor may know people from his previous job. I have worked for a variety of organizations, and it has been my experience that an advancement officer for one group who switches jobs may have a hard time bringing donors to the new organization. I am not saying it doesn't happen, but there are reasons beyond personal relations as to why a donor gives to a certain organization that do not apply to another. A serious donor to the University of Southern California likely will not make a large gift to the University of California at Los Angeles. If the organizations are complimentary and not competitors, a donor might follow an advancement officer for whom they have high regard.

It is often true that there are undiscovered gems in the list of prospects of an organization. If the organization has thousands of donors and prospects in their data base, it is impossible for all of them to be known to the advancement team. One time I worked for an organization that had a donor base of about 200,000 people who lived all over the United States. How is it possible to know who they are? No one can develop any kind of personal relations with 1,000 people much less 200 times that number. The same still applies if you whittle that down to 10,000 people who have given something in the last 18 months. Each organization is different, but probably no one can seriously manage relations with more than 250 in the best of circumstances.

I have seen in some organizations senior people with more than 1,000 prospects for whom they are responsible. The prospect manager is loathe, and loathe is not too strong a word, to give up 50 prospects to a new person who is just starting out. As one mentor explained to me earlier in my career, these relations are like little lambs with their shepherd. A new solicitor would be like the wolf trying to take them from his flock. But if these 50 people are not responding, and if they are not getting much personal attention, there should be no harm in shifting "shepherds." A new person needs to start somewhere. Often the CDO must step in and work out the reassignment of prospect managers. From the standpoint of the former solicitor, if the gifts come sometime in the future with a different assigned solicitor, he must see it as a good thing for the organization. The President of the non-profit will be happy to have a new donor. Depending on how much effort the former solicitor put in, he may claim a bit of the credit. It is just human nature to do so. It's a little like the person who tries and fails to twist open the lid on a jar and can't. He hands it to another who twists it off, and then claims "I loosened it up for you." Sure.

How Much Time Does It Take?

From the first contact a person has with an organization until the time there is a substantial donation, years might elapse. If a person is a newly hired solicitor for a non-profit, it likely will take time before he brings in results with a new contact. It takes longer if the solicitor is assigned to people who do not currently support the organization. It is probably a very good thing to have a clear understanding at the outset what expectations are about the first year of employment and the conditions of employment. How many prospects are assigned? Are any proven supporters, or are they people who have never given before and have had little contact with the organization? If a new solicitor is assigned to a few current or lapsed supporters, and the expectation is that they find new supporters, that must be considered. It is a general rule of thumb that the larger the gift the longer the cultivation period. The worst thing that a solicitor can exude is pressure to get prematurely a contribution when visiting with a potential donor. A six-figure gift may take five or six meetings before a donor would feel making such a gift is a good thing to do. It would be a shame if a premature ask results in a "no." A flat turn down is something to be avoided. Better to get a series of yeses on meetings, attending an event, maybe a lunch with a colleague, and a series of smaller gifts before going for the home run.

The other side is that the employer, as represented by the supervisor of the solicitor, is under pressure to show results. Nonetheless, a new solicitor is not going to get the same results as a person who has been soliciting gifts for an organization for five years. That is just the way it is.

Luck plays a role, though some people sometimes seem luckier than others. Perhaps luck is the wrong word. I recall a case where a donor had had contact with the President of a large non-profit more than thirty years earlier. There had been several CEOs since then. He sent in a check to the organization addressed to the widow of the long-deceased CEO for $1 million. A respected long-time solicitor of the organization that had a relation to the widow was assigned to this person. Many gifts followed. Everyone was happy, but I suspect none more than the current CEO and the assigned solicitor. The gifts were credited to the assigned advancement officer. You just never know. Thirty years.

WHAT IS FAIR COMPENSATION?

So, we come to the matter of compensation of advancement officers. What is fair? What keeps an advancement officer motivated to do his best for the organization and the donors?

I have been approached in the past by smaller organizations to work on a percentage basis. "We will give you 10% of whatever you bring in." I never liked the idea, and I have never accepted to work on that basis. The leader of the organization will say they would like to hire on a percentage basis because they just do not have the resources to pay a salary or a monthly retainer. It makes perfect sense to the leader because they, in fact, do not have the resources. If they know a person has been effective elsewhere in the past, they may think they could easily go to their contacts and ask. It would be, as they say, a "win-win." Is the motive of the solicitor to help further the charity, or is it simply to get the commission? And what of the ethical obligation to the organization for which they used to work? Might not a fundraiser working on a commission for a new organization be harming their previous employer by taking their supporters to another organization? Then there is the question of whether the new organization can deliver over time. What is the solicitor's obligation to see that the non-profit delivers? Suppose it is a small organization just starting out. Can they deliver what they promise? Furthermore, just because a solicitor was successful raising funds for one group, it does not mean he would be successful raising funds for another group.

Then there is the further question about next year's gift and the solicitor's relation to that donor. Who asks the donor a year later after giving the report to the donor on how the money was used? Same percentage for the second gift? And what of asking people who have given before to the organization over a period of years? Is the percentage the same? Who gets the commission? Suppose a friend of this faithful donor makes a gift? What then? If the donor knew that a gift of $100,000 would result in $10,000 going directly to the person who is asking, would they cheerfully give the check? If paid on a percentage basis, such a fundraiser really is raising the money, at least in part, for themselves. That may become the main concern. The fundraiser might not care so much about what was done with the money by the organization. All the donor knows is that a person has requested a $100,000 donation to go for a certain program, helping rescue abandoned dogs, or helping that veteran with no legs. The donor likely would not be told about the solicitor getting paid on a commission basis

It is far better for the organization to pay an agreed upon salary, or a retainer, rather than a commission. The advancement officer's job is to do his best to find donors and to ask them to help the organization. Further, he has a duty to the donor to make sure the organization follows through with the gift. The information in the 990 form does a fair job of giving the donor the lay of the land in terms of how much money goes for program, administration, and fundraising. Salaries of the officers and highly compensated individuals are included. Professional advancement officers do not receive compensation based on a commission. It is a bad recipe for the long-term success of the charity. It is for this reason that the Association of Fundraising Professionals have always adopted the standard that paying a solicitor on a percentage basis is unethical. It makes a lot of sense.

Referring to the 990 form, it is not a bad reference related to the matter of compensation. The 80-20 (Program, Fundraising, Administration) rule applies when it comes to approximating the compensation of an advancement officer. Gifts should be about five times greater than the salary and benefits of the solicitor in the first few years and, perhaps, thereafter ten times greater. Having written this formula, each organization is a bit different, and I cannot help but think of my experience as a young orange picker and caddy.

COMPARING COMPENSATION LEVELS

Suppose a solicitor has an outstanding year in terms of total dollars raised. He is paid the same as the person working at the same level who has a poor year by that same measure. What then? There is often the option of a bonus or a raise to recognize outstanding achievement when considering the performance over the whole year. But even here it is a subtle judgment. Let's say a solicitor named Dudley had many meetings with donors old and new. He was very good at moving many donors toward a gift in the future, but he did not do well the past year in terms of getting gifts in the bank. Meanwhile another solicitor, Lucky, obtained one large gift from one donor in the last year. Dudley may be laying the foundation for good years ahead, but did not have a good past year measured by gifts totals that came in. In effect Lucky was lucky, and Dudley had a good year as well, but was unable to reap the results.

These compensation decisions are tough. Usually there is someone who makes them. In a small organization, it may be the President. In a large organization, it likely would be the CDO. It is the CDO who is held accountable by CEO for the total funds raised and how much it cost to raise the gift totals. Sometimes a solicitor will also do public relations or some other function as well. If a CDO motivates all to be evaluated only on the total amount raised in a year, they might turn their happy band of solicitors into a pack of credit-claiming aggressors who make donors and their colleagues very uncomfortable. So, other metrics are needed as far as advancement is concerned. The number of meetings with donors that are completed; the number of proposals submitted and the amounts; the total number of gifts received from old and new donors, the total amount of all gifts, and such things are all important indicators of performance. There needs to be accountability based on gifts in the bank, but the performance measure must consider many factors.

From the standpoint of the solicitor, the healthiest attitude is to ignore, as much as humanly possible, their compensation level compared with anyone else. If advancement officers make a compensation agreement with an employer, they should stick by it and be happy with it. From my experience, I can say that no employer will ever think much of employees who state the salary of another person and, on that basis, say they should be compensated more. When that annual performance review comes up, a gift officer at some point states their case for the new year and the new compensation agreement. They should point out all they have done for the organization, including things that may not show up on whatever metrics the organization uses. If solicitors feel they are not being treated fairly, but they are not in a position financially to leave the organization, the best thing to do is polish up the resume and test the waters elsewhere. Have a plan B. I have found that people who continually compare themselves with others in terms of compensation are not going to be results oriented, and they are not people with whom I would like to work. Envy is not the way to build a career. It is so unpleasant as well.

There is another reason to have a plan B. Say a solicitor has had a series of good years, but the organization must cut back for reasons beyond their control. Its overall revenue is down, and belt tightening is required. It is possible that the organization might judge that the best way to carry on is to let a solicitor go. It is hard not to take it personally, but it might turn out well in the longer run. Always have a plan B.

Support for Advancement Officers

Another variable in the performance of a solicitor is the support they receive from the organization. It comes in many forms. If solicitors are to perform, they must have a budget. Budgets vary widely depending on the size of the organization. If it is a four-person shop, it is quite different than a college with its hundreds or even thousands of employees. Ideally the budget will cover all the following: business cards, office space, smartphone, computer, parking, mileage re-imbursement, client meetings, club dues, professional development, information concerning prospects, and information concerning operations, and priority projects of the organization along with related budgets. In addition to these, there is need for administrative assistance for answering telephones, scheduling appointments, solicitation letters and proposal production, invitation mailings, and data entry. Because of the advance of technology many of these office functions can be done by the advancement officers, but if they are out of the office visiting potential donors, or at organizational meetings, there is need for support. Fortunately, smart phones and computers can be synchronized with an administrative assistant. It is frequently the case that an administrative assistant will assist several solicitors.

A non-profit organization rarely will be able to provide all these support services unless there is reason to believe that they will result in donations that justify them. You will recall the 80-20 ratio spoken of earlier. The idea is that donation totals will be at least four times greater than the fundraising and the overall administrative expense of the organization. The non-profit CDO must weigh these variables with great care. Solicitors must also weigh them when they initially discuss employment with the non-profit. Exactly what kind of support might be reasonably given to do the job? It probably is also a good idea to discuss prospect assignments during the hiring process. If these things are left unsaid, in the weeks and months after hiring, solicitors may feel shortchanged regarding support when they compare themselves to others. As I mentioned earlier, it is not healthy to compare compensation levels with others, and the same is true for the levels of support. Nonetheless, it is only human nature to compare these very visible signs of support. The higher up a solicitor is in the organization, generally the greater the support budget. At the same time, there is an expectation for greater results.

RECORD KEEPING

If it has some level of sophistication, the organization will have software so that every contact with a donor or potential donor is recorded in the database that can be accessed by anyone on the advancement team. Raiser's Edge is a software program that is quite popular. There are others, and I have no doubt that in the future Raiser's Edge will have new iterations, or will be overtaken by some new kid on the block that offers more. However, conversion from one system to another is quite expensive and tedious.

Since people are different, there are variations in reporting. Some advancement officers put in the record an "action" item if they were in the same room with their assigned prospect in an unplanned "meeting." Others only record what they feel is a serious contact that was planned, and where a donation was discussed. If a donor is assigned to an advancement officer, the idea is that one person is responsible for managing the relation between the charity and the donor. It may be that another person has a previous relation and has some interactions that reveal important information. These too are placed in the record. Nonetheless, it is the prospect manager alone who is responsible for moving the donor along toward the best gift. The prospect manager is listed in the donor record so all who have access can see. If the donor is a board member, or a person of very high net worth "do not contact" protocols can be applied. This saves the donor from being contacted by different people who have access to the donor records.

If a donor has a history with the non-profit, the solicitor before the very first meeting should have studied that record with some care. Is there a record of correspondence? Have they attended events? If they have given money, surely there is previous correspondence. Are there reports of discussions about why the donor has an interest in the organization? Were there any adverse dealings in the past or sore subjects? Perhaps there is mention of a study or practice with which the donor took issue. Perhaps the donor had hoped for some development in the organization that had not yet taken place. Perhaps they still owe money on a past pledge. Why? The individual record should have such information. If solicitors have no knowledge of this, they fly blind and make a poor representation. There should be a record of a "thank you" letter for each past gift. There is also a section on relationships which is for relatives, friends, co-workers, and such. It is vital that all contact information such as home and business addresses, phones, emails, etc. be updated if there are changes.

If every donor only had a relationship with one person for the organization, the record keeping may seem less important, but memories do grow dim over time, especially if the solicitor is dealing with hundreds of people. Problems may arise when there are multiple people with contacts with the donor. If each person does his bit, the person responsible for the relationship will know how to proceed. And if the assigned solicitor moves on, the new person assigned will be able to carry on.

There is a need for policies of strict confidentiality about this information. It is often quite personal and it often involves people's assets and intentions about them. Maybe it involves a serious business set back, or a messy divorce, or any number of things. If a person learns that a donor has had an adverse turn of fortune, and they don't record it or report it to the appropriate advancement officer, it is possible that the solicitor might ask for that annual gift a few months later. Not good.

If board members learn of such things, they should pass it on to the CEO, or the CDO, and it is then incumbent on them to enter the information in the record. Sometimes, that can be sensitive. Suppose the CEO knows the vital information and thinks the information may be too personal to enter. In that case, the CEO needs at least to advise the CDO and the prospect manager, without going into the details, to lay off the donor for this cycle. Sensitive information needs to be registered with key people, if not in the record.

Because there are so many different demands on the CEO, it generally is not good practice for the CEO to be a prospect manager for donors. The problem is that while CEOs are the most important "witness for the case" for why a person should give, they are very busy people who have many responsibilities for the organization beyond development. Time and activities may intervene before the CEO has time to enter sensitive information. Human nature being what it is, the CDO cannot easily go to his boss and look him in the eye and ask him if he entered a report on the meeting, or if he asked this very important donor for that "end of the year" gift. The CDO would not want to be an irritating pest who has forgotten where he is in the pecking order. If the CEO wants to manage a relationship because he feels that it is worth it, the CDO should artfully encourage the CEO to record vital information and generally manage to make sure things are on track toward a gift. The CEO cannot hold the CDO responsible for raising money if he won't let him do his job to hold prospect managers accountable, even if it is the CEO. Both the CEO and the CDO need to be respectful of each other's role in the organization. In any successful organization, it is not a problem.

Because highly sensitive personal or business information needs to be recorded in the record of the donor, advancement officers and anyone with access to confidential donor records needs to realize the non-disclosure agreement (NDA) they signed when they were hired is a serious matter.

LOOK FOR WHAT IS MISSING

When gift officers are first hired to raise support for the organization, they should look for what is missing. Every organization is a work in progress, but if it has hired a new solicitor it means they want something more. Even if the new hire is a replacement, there is an opportunity to initiate.

For example, if the organization does not have a planned giving program, a new advancement officer should investigate what could be done to initiate or perhaps improve it. I went to work for a public policy research institute that did not have such a program. I wasn't even sure what such a program was and how it would work. I attended several planned giving seminars, and we began to place in-house ads in publications. We developed a stable of attorneys, and it began. The attorneys who specialize in estate planning frequently are asked by their clients if they know of a reputable charity. Eventually we had a Saturday morning seminar at no charge for people who were interested. It was very easy to recruit experts who could give attendees the latest on tax laws and estate planning. If attendees wanted to pursue the matters, they would know the expert who ran the seminar. It is wise to have a list of qualified experts from which prospects could choose. These gifts take time, but the results can be quite dramatic. Several large gifts came in after I had left the organization, but I felt good about getting that program started. Larger organizations might have an office run by a qualified attorney who specializes in estate planning and planned gifts.

Does the organization have an overseas travel program for advancement? I remember when I first proposed it for one organization the immediate response, in effect, was, "Oh, Mike wants a free trip to somewhere." So, I had to show that many organizations do such things to build closer relations with donors; that it could be self-funding; and that it would result in new contacts for the organization. I have introduced such programs to several different organizations. A point I would make is that when you talk to a person in his office and he is on one side of the desk and you are on the other for 45 minutes, it is not the greatest way to build a relationship of trust. Take a two-hour bus trip in a foreign location sitting next to someone, and the dynamics of that relation forever change. Even better if the bus breaks down and you all go through a crisis together. Well, I am not recommending a crisis, but if things happen along the way, and they do, they become shared memories that bind. If there are 30 people on a trip for ten days and it includes the husbands and wives, there are multiple opportunities each day to visit with supporters, learn about their lives, and build relations.

The trip should relate to the mission of the organization. Contrary to what some may think, such trips require effort and worry. Are the restaurants good? How expensive is the wine? Is there enough time for shopping? Is everyone on the bus with their luggage before the bus leaves the hotel? What about that couple that is always late and makes the whole bus wait? How is the lady who sprained her ankle getting around? How much time to allow from the hotel to the airport with customs, luggage, and immigration? What is the policy on tipping? Nonetheless, it is a great way to build relations.

Do advancement officers have memberships in local clubs? A membership at a local country club, even a social membership without court or golf course privileges, can be a good place to take people for lunch or to meet new prospects. Perhaps there is a local Rotary Club, Chamber of Commerce, World Affairs Council, or a university club that has speakers. These types of memberships are often reserved for the President or senior advancement officers. The higher up in the organization, the nicer the clubs. But even a club or association of a more modest price offers the opportunity to invite a prospect or to meet a new prospect. It shows the prospect, as well, that the organization has some regard for the advancement officer.

Is there an annual dinner? To be frank, dinners rarely raise money. In my experience, at best, they break even. But they do offer an opportunity for supporters and prospects to be briefed, or even inspired, about what is going on with the organization. Outstanding supporters can be publicly thanked. It provides opportunities to bring along new prospects. Supporters have a chance to visit with each other and to reinforce their commitment to the organization. If the speaker is a headliner, it may gain local media coverage. One organization I worked for had a very good foundation for such an event. A thoughtful donor gave an endowment gift that subsidized the annual dinner and an annual cash award for someone who spoke and who embodied for what the organization was known. Of course, we had to have an award committee to determine the recipient each year. That committee was also an outreach mechanism. While the endowment was not big enough to cover all the costs, it made it easier to at least break even. The event reinforced current supporters, and it also offered an opportunity to locate new supporters.

Many non-profits are lax on having a global advancement strategy. Universities, colleges, think tanks, churches, scientific organizations and others increasingly engage citizens from other countries. Businesses of consequence must have a global strategy. International students attend colleges and universities. Think tanks who study US foreign policy will frequently have dealings with scholars and officials from other countries. Churches often have overseas missions. Scientists will increasingly deal with counterparts in other countries. Disaster-relief organizations frequently support efforts overseas. While there are these dealings overseas, often there is not much thought or commitment given to raising funds overseas. A wealthy Japanese citizen may wish to have presence and participation in the research of a public policy think tank in Washington, DC. A wealthy family who lives in China might wish to make a gift to a university that has graduated several of its members. It might give the family some prestige back home to have an endowed professorship or a building bearing their name. An international donor might make an excellent member of the Board of Directors. Perhaps a wealthy person in India is interested to foster legal collaboration between institutions in the area of dispute resolution so that arbitration or mediation might be utilized to resolve disputes rather than expensive civil litigation. World Vision, International Committee for the Red Cross, Doctors Without Borders are a few non-profits with a global vision who must have a global advancement strategy.

In addition to the Board of Directors, might the organization develop an Advisory Board that would be a consultative body? Membership would require an annual higher dollar gift as well as attendance at quarterly or semi-annual meetings with the President in exchange for the prestige of being listed in the annual report and on the website. The mission of such a board would vary depending on the geographic reach of the organization. We have discussed earlier the merits of having estate attorneys, CPAs, and Certified Financial Planners affiliated with the group to meet periodically. One thing to keep in mind about

Advisory Boards is that they may give advice. Does the non-profit act on it or not? The more formalized the structure of an Advisory Board, the more likely it will want to be taken seriously.

If the charity is large enough with a substantial endowment fund, it might be wise to ask donors if they would like to set up the previously described Donor Advised Fund (DAF) that is managed by the charity. Donors can take a large charitable exemption that possibly could be spread out over several years. They retain the ability to direct gifts to charities they like, assuming they are qualified. They do not have to worry about laws and rules governing charitable foundations. The charity assumes responsibility for managing the assets. And, there is a possibility that in time the fund could become a gift to the charity. This should not be done unless the scale of the charity's endowment is considerable. Strict accounting standards and reporting need to be maintained.

New advancement officers should look around to see what is missing when they start out with an organization. What might be added? What might be improved? Is there some existing program that needs tweaking to be more effective?

TIME MANAGEMENT

Probably one of the most important factors in the success of advancement officers is knowing the best use of their time. Spending time with donors or potential donors is without a doubt the best use of time. It is how a solicitor learns more about the hopes and intentions of the prospect. What do they value most? Whether it be a cup of coffee in a prospect's office, a conversation over lunch, sitting together at an event, or playing some tennis, time with a donor is the most important thing.

I always make a habit of reading newspapers or watching television news. It helps in conversations, but it is something I am interested in anyway. I also like reading and ideas. All these activities make it easier to talk with a donor.

When a solicitor's head hits the pillow at night, they should have their appointment schedule in mind for the next day. They should envision what they wish to accomplish at their meetings and what information handout they might need to bring along.

All the information in the records of prospects should have been gone through by the time of the meeting so there is clarity about where the solicitor is in moving the prospect along. It may be that a prospect isn't ready for a gift. That is OK. In fact, it is important to know. It never hurts to make friends with anyone along the way. The future is a mystery and sometimes help comes from the unexpected. Besides, a person who is not interested in your charity now, may know someone who might be. People might have other priorities, and that is part of what makes the world go around.

Inevitably in large non-profits, there are meetings for the advancement team. Meetings should have a printed agenda along with a start time and an end time. They are necessary so that members of the team may know where matters stand with the organization, learn the current priorities, hear developments about an upcoming event, receive advance information on an upcoming public announcement, hear some success stories from peers, and report any difficulties that might be of common concern. These meetings should be a help to the solicitor when he meets his prospects. If general meetings become a mere logistical feat with a good dose of office politics, they need to be re-evaluated. Meetings are not an end in themselves.

PERFORMANCE REVIEW

There is also need for a monthly or quarterly meeting between a solicitor and his supervisor where there is a review of results, successes, problems, and things that might be done by the organization to help achieve the understood goals. At the same time, the supervisor might notice some things about how a gift officer is going about his job that could be improved. Perhaps changes in prospect assignments can be reviewed. These meetings need not be long, but they are important.

Annual performance reviews are more serious for the solicitor and the supervisor. They should not be pro-forma exercises. Having a whole series of boxes in different areas of performance to check off where a person is given an "excellent," "good," "satisfactory," or "unsatisfactory" on some such scale can be very impersonal and not helpful. In fact, these can be dispiriting if the supervisor simply shows the advancement officer the boxes checked, and asks for their signature to indicate they have read it. Usually there is opportunity to register any comments. If the performance metrics concerning money raised, donor visits, and proposals submitted are wrong, they need to be corrected. If there are other achievements not noted that benefit the organization, they need to be brought up. If there are things the organization could do to help increase donations, they should be discussed. "Shows initiative," "gets along well with others," "shows attention to detail," and such have an element of subjectivity without specific references. They can be based on third hand conversations and impressions and are really not helpful without specificity.

Most importantly, there is a need to agree upon goals going forward. If a person is not reaching their goals, the question is why not? Are the goals appropriate? Do they challenge, or are they simply unrealistic for the next cycle? Perhaps in the first year, that 80-10-10 ratio formula is unrealistic. Is it realistic the next year? If not, why not? If a person achieves dollar amounts way above the goals, then a raise or bonus should be in order. Frequently, there is an institutional salary increase to meet inflation. If the average for the advancement department is 2%, and a solicitor is considerably below the goal, well there is a chance the 2% is not in the cards. If a person is above the goal, then perhaps a raise over the 2% is merited. Advancement officers can read the 990 forms too as they consider their worth to the organization. These are serious matters. In addition to individual performance the relative health of the organization, especially regarding fundraising, will be important considerations for compensation.

Specificity and good will are required on both sides of this important annual conversation to help raise funds to accomplish the mission of the cause.

CHAPTER VIII

Other Sources of Support

FOUNDATIONS

RAISING FUNDS FROM A LARGE CHARITABLE FOUNDA-TION is quite different than raising funds from an individual. For one thing, by looking at their annual 990 filing you can learn much about the size of the foundation's assets and to what they give money and in what amounts. They usually have a website where they state their purpose, the types of programs they support, and their requirements to consider a proposal. These all need to be studied with care. Note should be made of who is on the Board as there might be an ally. If an organization fits, then the solicitor follows the requirements in terms of what information they need. Though it is true that an empathetic and positive personality is always a plus, there is no getting around the matter of a proper fit.

Usually the foundation will want to have a detailed plan and budget for the use of the money by the non-profit. They also may want a copy of the founding articles of incorporation, the by-laws, the most recent 990 form, and the most recent audited financial statement. There are variations among foundations. They may request a variety of information that is in these documents and that it be put in a certain order in the format they require. They may state up front that they cannot give more than, say, an amount of money greater than 10% of the overall budget for the organization. Some foundations will be clear and say they only give support to educational and scientific organizations. If the solicitor represents a private K-8 school, however great the need and exemplary the performance, there is no point in asking. Some foundations will say they only give to capital campaigns to build a structure for non-profits. Others will say just the opposite. Some will say they do not accept unsolicited applications for grants, but only when they request an application. In this case, there needs to be some conversation in advance by the foundation leadership and a program officer or a high-ranking executive within the non-profit seeking the grant.

Some foundations will only accept proposals from January through March of the calendar year. If the proposal arrives in May, it shows that the applicant is careless and does not respect the foundations procedures. Some foundations receive a massive number of requests and the officers who work for them immediately look to see which proposals they can throw out right away. Some foundations state up front that they do not have time to reply to reply to each application. Another "no-no" for the applicant is to apply again too soon after the last rejection.

Let's assume that the foundation accepts an application for $400,000 to be paid over four years. They require an annual accounting of the accomplishments each year and how much money was spent. After receiving the report and approving it, they will release the second payment. Usually, while a non-profit is in this four-year term, it cannot apply for any other grant until the earlier grant is fulfilled. After the term is finished, the cycle can begin again.

If a charity has ten different grants in play, someone needs to be the key person in charge to know where matters stand with each application and with the reporting requirements. There cannot be multiple requests going in to the same foundation. The person in charge of foundation relations also needs to know which foundation should be sending in a check and when it should arrive. Therefore, general advancement officers must defer to the person on the advancement team who is responsible for foundations. This person's skill set is different than a general advancement officer. It requires an attention to detail and process management that has different requirements than a person skilled at one-on-one cultivation and relationship building.

Experts or professors may know better than advancement officers which foundation may be appropriate for a grant. The reason is simple. If specialists have worked for 25 years in a field like bio-chemistry or development issues in South America, they likely will have had dealings with the XYZ Foundation in the past. It is also possible that they may know the experts at the foundation who specialize in the field. So, there is need for collaboration between the expert and the advancement officer of the non-profit about how to proceed with the targeted foundation. Advancement officers need to understand that specialists need space in crafting the case for a grant to the foundation. Specialists need to realize that advancement officers have the responsibility to make sure the proposal meets all the requirements for the application; reports are given according to the deadlines; and the final report at the end of the grant is done in a timely fashion. Foundation advancement officers also need to be a traffic cop to avoid multiple grant applications from different experts so they do not compete with one another. In case there are multiple ideas for a grant from the same foundation, the non-profit needs to go with its strongest application.

Some smaller family foundations may work differently than the larger foundations. It may be that the person that set it up keeps things simple. Rather than a complex division of labor within the foundation, they may behave almost like a wealthy individual donor. They do need to avoid a failure to give away less than the 5% federal minimum requirement for grants. Sometimes at the end of the year they may be scrambling a bit to give away money. In the case of a small family foundation run by the donor who is the foundation's CEO, the relationship management may best be served by a regular advancement officer rather than advancement officer who specializes in foundations. These are judgment calls best worked out between the respective advancement officers and, if need be, the CDO.

CORPORATIONS AND CORPORATE FOUNDATIONS

Frequently the advancement officer that handles proposals and plays traffic cop for foundations is the same person who manages relations with corporations or corporate foundations. Corporations that try to build good will in the community also have corporate interests. They may fund conferences or research that furthers a corporate agenda while at the same time helping a non-profit that seeks the public good. The corporate public affairs office must exercise good judgment as does the entity that receives the donation lest the donation be perceived as only a benefit to the corporation and not the public good.

In the 1970s in Washington, DC there was a non-profit public policy organization that emerged called the Committee for the Clear and Present Danger. Its mission was to counter what was perceived to be an aggressive Soviet arms build-up during the Cold War. Its leadership was composed of well-known former public officials who were respected across the political spectrum. The organization adopted a policy that more than 50% of its funding had to come from sources other than those companies that produced weapons. Further, they adopted the policy that of those companies that did produce weapons, they could contribute no more than 5% of the total revenue. In this way their studies, conferences, and publications would have more credibility.

It doesn't take much imagination to see how good judgment on the part of the donor and the recipient is vital. If Apple Inc. was the sole funder of research on a publication on national security and the use of mobile phones, there is a direct corporate interest involved. Corporations that are in the areas of pharmaceuticals, oil and gas, solar energy, agriculture, insurance, finance, etc. have fiduciary responsibilities to their shareholders and customers. So, any non-profit needs to consider their own reputation and how the support might look to their mission and their constituents they serve. They need to ensure that the support from the corporations does further the mission of the non-profit. If they are not prudent, they may turn off supporters of their cause who

are needed. This business approach is farmed out to an appropriate financial institution.

An "endowment campaign" seeks to build up investable permanent funds for the long-term success of the organization. Perhaps there is need for a new medical capability for a hospital and it requires funding above and beyond the regular activities of the hospital. A think tank may wish to fund a permanent research position in a public policy area. Perhaps a college wants to increase its endowed scholarship funds, the endowed chairs for its current professors, or for professors it wishes to attract. If successful, it will attract a better quality of professor or student. Endowment funds are to be permanent and to serve a stated purpose that is intrinsic to the organizations mission.

There is also what is called a "comprehensive campaign." This is a campaign to raise total dollars in a set period. Such a campaign includes both annual gifts as well as gifts for the endowment or funds for capital projects. Comprehensive campaigns naturally have a little less focus since they combine both annual gifts, gifts to the endowment targeted for certain programs, or capital gifts for buildings and other fixed assets.

There is a specialized art to campaigns and frequently non-profits will engage outside consultants to provide advice. The most immediate question to ask is: What is the goal? That target goal should fit in with the mission and long-range strategy of the organization. It makes no sense to raise money because it's there for the taking. Additionally, the organization should establish a financial goal that is a stretch, but that is not beyond the realm of possibility. Most any organization would like more resources so why aren't they always in a campaign with a very high dollar amount? Human nature being what it is, organizations, like people, have habits. There should be a good reason to go into campaign mode, because the organization is saying to the current donors and the broader community that now is a special time. Supporters must dig deeper than usual and here are the reasons why that is so. A charity can't declare a campaign every day. It must make the case for this special campaign. It is not business as usual. As is true for all manner of advancement efforts, the CEO is the ultimate witness for the case for the campaign.

PLANNING PHASE

The President and the Board of Directors must be enthusiastically supportive of the idea for the campaign. The CEO, after consulting key leadership, must present a general vision of what the organization could do with this extra $1 million, or $100 million dollars, or whatever is presented. What would the organization become with these new gifts? If the Board gives the green light, there then is a need to go through a more rigorous strategic planning process. The key leadership and program leaders are asked for what they need funds. They check with all in their respective domains to learn their hopes and dreams. Each department makes a list of all they need in terms of space, personnel, equipment and such things to accomplish goals that would advance the mission. Maybe there is a vital need for a new department. Existing department heads make their best estimates as to costs within their area. They put in rank order what is most important for their future success. Others in finance check the figures to see if they are in the ballpark of reality. This more complete picture is presented to the Board for their thoughts. Refinements are made. Then, cue the consultant.

Generally, a group will put the campaign consulting part out for bid. These are firms that have much experience in guiding campaigns for different kinds of organizations. If a firm does this work over time, it will have developed an expertise that is quite specialized. It is good to have an outsider who has no departmental favorites or interests involved as to the campaign plan. Campaign consultants provide another reality check. So, the CDO, perhaps the President, and maybe even a board member will interview consultants and obtain bids from them.

Depending on the consultant, they will conduct at the minimum a feasibility study to determine what is a reasonable campaign goal. The

Board may collectively like the idea of the campaign, but then there is the question of how much each person on the Board would be willing to give above and beyond what they currently give. Which parts of the proposed campaign especially excites them? Which part do they think has little merit? The consultant requests confidential one-on-one meetings with board members. This guarantee of confidentiality assures that if a board member was too timid to express a contrary view in a regular board meeting, he could do so to the consultant. Perhaps it is just that upon further reflection a few weeks later they have another thought. How much would the board member be prepared to give above their normal annual contribution? Or, perhaps the question is asked about what is a range of what they could give, above their normal support, over the life of the campaign. Some campaigns are five years, give or take.

After talking to the board members, especially those that are vital in terms of financial support, the consultant then speaks with key staff to get a sense of things. They speak with some of the leading advancement officers. They then ask to interview the important existing donors to the organization as to what they might wish to do for the campaign after hearing the general outline and seeing some of the preliminary plan. This is a bit nerve wracking for the CEO and the development officers because this outsider is talking to some of the most important funding sources the organization has been nurturing and on whom they depend. Again, confidentiality is assured. It is a very good exercise as sometimes constructive ideas are uncovered as well as possible new donor levels. Then too, pitfalls to be avoided may be uncovered.

Next the consultant talks in confidence to a group of high net worth potential donors who are involved a little with the organization, but who could do more. The consultant again asks if they might be interested to support any aspect of the plan. Lastly, the consultant will meet in confidence with wealthy people in the community who are not involved with the organization. What do they think about the organization and this proposed plan? He may uncover some supporters, or he may uncover specific reasons why these people do not support the organization.

Armed with the feedback he gains from these meetings, the campaign consultant will report back to the CEO and the CDO, and the campaign plan will be further refined. Perhaps he might discover the plan should be more, or maybe less, ambitious than originally thought. Maybe the report will be that there is very little interest in some aspect of the campaign. The staff leadership then has a task to take this new information into account and refashion the strategic plan accordingly.

The consultants, depending on the capabilities of the organization, can leave the execution all to the organization. On the other hand, they may be helpful in creating brochures, a campaign timetable, and planning meetings with key campaign volunteer leaders and staff to discuss campaign donor prospects. Getting volunteers who are supporters of the organization is vital, since they can recruit peers to join in. The exact services of the consultants depend upon the Request for Proposal to which they initially responded with a bid. They might offer advice along the way.

The one last piece to this planning stage is to create the gift pyramid. There are various rules of thumb about campaign "pyramids" of support. At the very top of the pyramid is the lead gift. This is the largest gift needed to make the goal. In the second row are the lesser, but still quite large gifts. In the third row, large gifts, and so on. When making this pyramid, the campaign staff needs to have a pyramid that equals the gift total. Perhaps that last row is the number of $1,000 donors. At the very bottom is all the rest of the gifts. It is not just a mathematical exercise. Names need to be added to the list of potential supporters at the various levels. How many potential donors at each level are needed to make the goal? What is the assumed gift total from staff, especially the advancement staff?

Another rule of thumb is that for every gift needed in that pyramid, there is need to have four names to ask. If your batting average is .250, then the campaign is doable. Obviously in some ways this is highly theoretical. You may have some advancement officers who want to show enthusiasm in a session to create a pyramid. Solicitor Olivia Optimist may believe that half of her prospects are willing to give 50% of their estimated net worth for the campaign, whereas solicitor Patrick Pessimist believes that he would be lucky if his 5% prospects would give 1% of their net worth. Olivia would be sitting in the front row smiling and shooting up her hand at each level of the pyramid as names are put forward. Patrick would be in the back row, looking a little grumpy at the whole exercise. Patrick might be the most successful advancement officer in the history of the organization, but he really doesn't like these meetings! The CDO and the campaign consultant would be trying to gage what is real and would never want to quash enthusiasm. You want to stretch the organization, but you do not want to fail to achieve the goal. In fact, it would be very good to exceed your goal.

QUIET PHASE

Now, you have the Board, the CEO, key staff, and the circle of closer major donors and possible donors, thinking seriously about the campaign. You have a long list of names organized by gift-giving potential and likelihood. Solicitors are assigned to each potential donor. You now enter what is called the "quiet phase." Well, the previous phase was quiet too. The point is there is no publicity given out yet by the organization to the broader community. The key need in this phase is to work to gain hard commitments and gifts at various levels of support.

Perhaps the most important matter for the success of the campaign is the selection of the campaign Chair or Chairs, the Honorary Chair or Chairs, and the Leadership Committee. It is quite common for the lead gift, the one that sets the standard, to be 10% of the campaign goal. This means if the goal is $1 million, the lead gift is $100,000. If the campaign goal is $100 million, then that lead gift needs to be $10 million. It is at this point that the organization goes into its "we are special and different" dance. Maybe so. Perhaps there are two people who will pledge up front that they will give 5% over the life of the campaign. It may be that the lead gift giver does not want the title of Chair. Nonetheless, serious thought needs to be given about what the organization expects by way of a personal gifts and solicitation activity from each of these campaign leaders.

If you have a well-known board member or two who command the attention of the community and they are publicly identified as campaign leaders, they must lead in gift giving. If they do not commit to give the largest gifts in the 5-10% range of the total, you should not name them to the position. The reason is simple. If they do not give the largest gifts of the campaign, they cannot exert more direct influence on their friends, or indirect influence on others, to give. Others toward the top of the pyramid in rows two and three, especially board members, will take their cue from those above them in the gift pyramid. Campaign leaders must lead. The dynamic is like the vigorous downward stroke of a water pump that pulls up the water. A weak downward stroke won't pull up much water. A large gift by the campaign leadership tells more capable donors that this campaign is exceptionally important, and they need to dig deep. It is good to have at least four viable candidates for these very large gifts at the top of the gift pyramid. Pledges and donations are to be made before the public phase of the campaign begins. The pledged amount should be paid by a date certain. The general rule of thumb is to have pledges, or gifts, in hand for about 50% of the campaign before going public. Once the advancement team hits that magic number, the organization is then ready for the public phase.

PUBLIC PHASE

This is the time for public fanfare. Kick off events are held. Perhaps a media event is held, or a video is released on social media. Visual reference is made on the website. Brochures are sent out; personalized visits are made; letters on special campaign stationery requesting support are sent out; and the advancement staff at all levels kicks into high gear to make the other 50%. Advancement staff accompany board members and campaign leadership on visits to prospects. When a potential donor is approached, they might think that the amount of money is huge, but they may be reassured and encouraged to know that the organization is already half-way there with support from people who are impressive. The idea is that prospects will reappraise the importance of the organization, and that the campaign will induce them to come along and join the band wagon with a generous gift. Perhaps this phase of the campaign goes for another three years. Establishing a deadline is a bit of a gamble. Having the deadline can spur donors to make specific commitments by a date certain. So, a deadline is needed. Suppose you achieve the goal a year before the campaign is scheduled to end? In this happy turn of events, you can add to the goal for that last year and explain that there were items not originally on that initial list that were vital, but that the organization thought too ambitious. Success breeds success.

There could be another problem. Suppose, as the initial deadline looms, the charity is woefully short. What then? That deadline needs to be moved back and the campaign needs to be extended until the goal is met. Moving back the deadline requires some artful public communication. Any organization that launched the public phase of their campaign in the spring of 2008, were faced with the financial debacle in the fall of 2008. Recalibration would have been understandably called for after a meeting with the campaign leadership committee. Any number of circumstances might occur that cause moving back the date of completion. Perhaps the CEO dies, or gets a once-in-a-lifetime offer to leave and go elsewhere. In any case, postponing the deadline is sometimes necessary.

When the goal is met, the grand finale is a closing banquet giving thanks to all who have helped to make the campaign a success. Campaign Chairs are especially honored. A program lists those who gave at the various levels and they are recognized and thanked. Key leaders speak on what the campaign means for the organization in terms of achieving its strategic goals.

COUNTING AND MOPPING UP

There is sometimes a difference between achieving campaign goals and the revenue that is shown on the books. It doesn't mean there is anything nefarious going on. There are some very specific requirements for showing revenue on the audited financial statement. If a donor puts a bequest in a will for a certain amount of money as part of the campaign, can the charity count it? The campaign may count it, but the corporate treasurer will not. Why? It is possible that the would-be donor changes his mind. It is also possible that he suffers a horrendous financial setback, and he doesn't have the money. Another possible example is that a donor makes a three-year signed pledge agreement to make three payments each year. Suppose he signs this agreement in the last year of the campaign, but then he too suffers a setback and he cannot make the 3rd payment. The treasurer must put in a footnote to the next audited financial statement to explain why the assets have changed. There are also other types of gifts, planned gifts covered in Chapter V, that are counted differently. Immediately after the campaign, the advancement staff needs to pitch in and follow up on all those uncollected pledges made.

BEGIN AGAIN

When the campaign is over, in the back of the mind of the CDO, the general contours of the next campaign are beginning to grow. He and the President keep it to themselves. It is vital to re-assess what kind of organization now exists. It should be quite different than when the campaign began. New supporters will have emerged. New capabilities will be present. New opportunities will have emerged. After a decent interval when the new normal is established, it is then that the early planning stages for the next campaign should begin.

CHAPTER X
The Personal Ask

S O, AN ADVANCEMENT OFFICER OF A NON-PROFIT has been assigned to some prospects. They have done their research. How do they ask donors for a gift? For how much do they ask? There are so many variables to consider in answering these questions. Below is a series of questions to consider. To make it clear, I have never known the answers to all these questions for any donor. Some of the answers briefly cover matters already discussed in more detail. Advancement officers should not spend all their time at their desk learning every detail about a person's life before asking for a gift. In fact, the donor may know quite a bit about the organization already, and they may have an idea of what they want to do before they ever meet a solicitor. The questions below apply in about the same way whether a donor is a man or a woman. People are complex. Each person is unique and in particular circumstances that can change over time. These questions are not the type of thing a gift officer sits down over dinner and asks a donor. Further, no one answer determines a specific course of action in the process. There are always exceptions.

This section is for solicitors so that they are able to ask a donor for a gift that is appropriate. A donor might cringe a bit at these questions. Nonetheless, when a donor talks to his accountant, attorney, or certified financial planner, this type of information is helpful when crafting a will, a living trust or setting up a retirement plan. The same holds true for a responsible advancement officer of a charity who is going to ask for a major gift.

How wealthy is the prospect?

The wealth of the prospect is obviously very important. What is their net worth? As mentioned earlier, there are a variety of ways to get an idea about wealth, whether it be through an Internet search or a wealth ratings service. Still it isn't always possible to have a clear picture. If a donor has a net worth of $100 million, it is quite different than if they have a net worth of $500,000. The same thing applies related to annual income. I knew a donor who had a net worth considerably more than $1 billion. For a good number of years, they gave $2,500 at the end of the year. Several of my colleagues were disappointed. They did not realize that this billionaire donor was an accountant at heart, and was notorious for watching their donations with great zeal. As I told my associates, this person would not give one penny if they did not think we were a good charity worthy of support. Someone of enormous wealth is worth cultivating over time so that they begin to trust the organization and those that represent it. Above all else, it is good to learn what they find worthy of support and excel in those things if it fits in within the strategic planning of the organization. Have a plan that would appeal to this person so that your non-profit could compete with his other charitable interests, or add a new dimension to them. At least by knowing in a general sense a person's net worth, it helps an advancement officer know what a donor could do if motivated. That is the challenge.

Does the prospect give indication of a charitable tendency?

A potential donor may be quite wealthy, but if he is not inclined to support worthwhile charities it may be a bridge too far. On the other hand, a person may not be nearly as wealthy as some, but they may be inclined to support worthwhile causes. It is important to know what other causes a donor has supported. Some donors are quite disciplined and may only support causes in a certain field. Others may have defined several fields of interest. What are they? Charities often publish in annual reports, dinner programs and such publications lists of supporters at various levels. These are also indicators of reasonable target gift amounts. The information is not dispositive however. Life situations change. Also, the degree of enthusiasm for one cause may not be the same for another. Nonetheless, if a development officer knows a person does give, it is very helpful in approximating the amount and specific purpose of the ask.

What is the age of the prospect?

An older person generally is more apt to be able to make a substantial gift than a younger person. The children have left the nest. The donor has accumulated what they need to survive. It is true that sometimes a wealthy parent will set up a trust for a child and at any early age a charitably inclined younger person might participate in charitable giving. That is not common, but I know of some cases. A person in their 80s who has retired knows that the candle wick is starting to burn a little lower. If they have more than enough to provide for themselves and if their children and grandchildren are on track, they are more likely than many to make a substantial gift.

Is the older prospect still active in employment or business?

If a person is in their 60s or 70s, in good health, and is still working or actively investing their assets, they are still accumulating wealth, or maybe they are paying off some serious debt. In any case, if they are actively increasing their wealth, they may still be of a mindset to accumulate rather than make a legacy gift. Still, if they are well to do, they may enjoy the involvement that comes with annual giving and involving themselves in the good works of a charity. Board membership might be of interest, or perhaps a planned gift.

What is the prospect's family situation?

If the donor is married, it is very important to know the feelings and beliefs of the spouse related to a possible gift, especially if it is a large gift. Is the spouse supportive or reluctant? Any gift officer must appreciate both the husband and the wife for a major gift even though only one may seem to be the main driver of gift. Both are donors. Usually, the spouse is supportive, but not always. The spouse is also an important factor when considering the size of a gift as the spouse will want to be assured that they are going to be taken care of in subsequent years. This is especially so if the spouse is significantly younger than the donor. Some of the planned gifts mentioned earlier can be based on two lives so that a younger spouse will feel secure in making the gift. Sometimes the spouse of the more visible donor has wealth independent of the donor.

If a donor has been married several times, this may become a complicating factor since the obligations to the former spouse or the children from a previous marriage may be considerations that influence the size of any charitable gift. Obligations from divorce settlements can restrict a donor's desire and capacity to give. Trust the donor's judgment on these matters, but be mindful that he may have considerations that limit his capacity to give.

Children are always a consideration in any significant gift. A donor who makes a large gift to a charity may be perceived as taking money from the children because of the rules of inheritance. If there is careful planning in a larger estate, planned gifts can be made that are a win for the charity and a win for the children. The loser in these plans is the federal government. Usually in these types of matters, the children are older. Some children will do better in life and wealth creation than others. If a child is 50 years old and feeling life has not been fair to him, he may not want to see his older parents making a charitable gift that would affect his inheritance. Another child of about the same age who has a successful career may not feel threatened by the parent making a sizable bequest or outright gift. It is also possible a child may even need life-long care.

Children in a blended family may not feel they have been treated properly. These family considerations, as well, may weigh heavily on a donor, and are important to understand. Again, finally, it is the judgment of the donor that is paramount. For future relations it is good to have the children on board if possible. Just as easily it could be that the parents introduce the children to a charity, and the second generation enjoys following their parents' footsteps in helping an organization. That is an occasion to celebrate the several generations of support from such a family. It is always good to appreciate the children and to have and to show interest in them. What makes them tick?

What is the nationality or ethnicity of the prospect?
Increasingly, especially in California, New York and other major entrepots in the United States, we have citizens who have come from other countries who can give. I have met advancement officers who feel native born Americans are more generous than other nationalities. Likely it is just that they do not feel as comfortable with someone of a different ethnicity. That type of mentality needlessly limits the prospects for gift-giving.

A person from an Asian country, for example, may revere higher education more than a typical American, if there is such a thing as a typical American. They also might have a feeling of loyalty to their alma mater that exceeds a typical American. I have also seen instances where this feeling of loyalty translates into the next generation. Further, in some cultures a major gift to a university or a major charity conveys a status to their peers that is much more important to them than those from another culture.

Anyone who has come to America and been successful in term of wealth creation will often feel enormous satisfaction at being able to help those less fortunate. Joining the philanthropic community can be a matter of pride as well. Those same feelings motivate anyone, but especially someone who has come to this country and achieved great success financially. Let me give an example. There is an important opera in a large metropolitan city in the southwest that has a variety of types of donor groupings. One is for people of Hispanic, or Latino, heritage. A lady on the committee that I knew wanted to let the broader community know that many of her heritage had a sophisticated appreciation for opera and a capacity to support it. She felt strongly about making that statement.

It would be well to be conversant in the history, religion, and culture of any potential donor. It shows respect. Corporate gifts from businesses based elsewhere in the world may also be a way to enhance the company's global brand. These types of corporate gifts have a different dynamic to them, but these sources will have increasing importance in philanthropy that takes place in the United States.

Is the prospect in good health?

If there is a severe health problem, the donor may be wanting to "get his affairs in order." On the other hand, the donor may feel that he may need his assets to pay for prolonged medical treatment or assisted living care. Usually persons who are older have insurance of some sort that would cover most illnesses. I knew a person in his 70s who worried about everything going wrong and he just could not make a substantial gift despite having a significant net worth. He had gone through the Great Depression and WWII. These experiences may affect people who fear being left penniless. Wealth for some is a great comfort. Others may find comfort in the love of their children and grandchildren, their friends, and a community. Usually it is a mix.

Past bouts with cancer or some other debilitating and life-threatening illnesses will influence a person's feeling about giving. It could let them know the clock is ticking, and it is time to make that gift that leaves a legacy. It might also point them in a direction to donate to research to prevent people in the future from having the same disease.

Is the prospect of sound mind?

An advancement officer should not be asking a donor for a gift who is in early dementia, or who has some sort of mental problem. This is especially true if a spouse or children are involved. Sometimes children, a spouse, or a relative will take a charity to court for exercising undue influence on a person who is not of sound mind. That is about the last thing a charity would want. It harms their reputation, and it costs money to defend in court. Better to back off, or to have the conversation with the spouse or children who may know best what is the intention of the donor. It is optimal that a donor makes their plans in advance of any mental deterioration, and that their family members are informed of this as well as their estate planning professionals.

How did the prospect accumulate his wealth?

Some people accumulate their wealth by keen analytical skills and sharp investing. This would be the typical "green eyeshade" kind of person. A calculator. Maybe the calculator would like the leverage a dollar-for-dollar challenge gift would create. On the other hand, another may have accumulated wealth by sales, contacts, being active in the community and in ways that are more social. Bearing in mind all the previous factors, it could be that the donor with the more social style of wealth accumulation may feel an obligation to "give back.' Or it could even be that board members of your cause have played a role in this potential donor's accumulation of wealth.

Is the wealth liquid or illiquid?

If a person has adequate resources to make a gift and has his resources in money market funds, or some such liquid account, writing a check is a simple matter. That is rare. Suppose his wealth is in real estate, a business, or stocks? A donor may be wealthy but in no position to write a check. As mentioned earlier, gifts of stocks or highly appreciated assets offer a chance to bypass capital gains and result in a charitable deduction. Appreciated assets as discussed earlier are excellent for a Charitable Gift Annuity, a Charitable Remainder Uni-Trust, or a straight gift of the assets. Usually people have a mix of liquid and illiquid assets. Gifts of real estate may be problematic since there may be environmental hazards for which your cause might be liable. Are property taxes up to date? Are there any outstanding claims? Due diligence is required for gifts of real estate, but such gifts can be quite significant.

What is the prospect's politics? Republican? Democrat? Other?

If the person is interested in your organization and it has little to do with politics, there is no need to talk about any politics. Many of the causes I represented have been conservatively oriented. The politics of a donor in these instances are important. I have learned the fine distinctions between traditional Conservatives, Libertarians, Paleo-Conservatives, Neo-Conservatives, big-government conservatives, West Coast Straussians, East Coast Straussians, and others. If a gift officer is working for a liberal oriented cause, no doubt he should know in detail those fine distinctions on that side of things. Either way, a solicitor should look for donors in the same ballpark for the organization he represents. In addition, such a donor may have a history with some of these think tanks or publicly elected officials. It may be important to know if they are Republican, Democrat, or one of the minor parties. Emphasize whatever it is in your cause that is close to the donor's heart. If politics is unrelated to the mission of the organization you represent, do not bring it up.

Raising funds at a university is quite different. Universities tend to be liberal in many respects, though they do tend to shy away from elective or legislative politics. Well, they are supposed to do so. Most alumni are less liberal than the faculties. It is important to find whatever the fundraiser can that might appeal to that potential donor that is going on at the university. Many alumni simply have a warm feeling for alma mater and would simply like to make a gift. If it is to be a big gift, that is where the gift officer needs to know aspects of the university where the donor could make a gift with strategic impact. Though a bit more complicated, perhaps the results-oriented advancement officer could work with the Dean, or the department head, to craft a gift plan that would please the donor and improve the academic quality of the university in a meaningful way.

At the very least, a good advancement officer needs to be sensitive to the political orientation of the donor, lest by an inadvertent comment he turn-off that potential donor.

Has the donor supported certain political parties, candidates or initiatives?
If you are raising money for a candidate, or in support of legislation or an initiative, perhaps the most important thing to know is the person's giving history. These are all available on a variety of websites. Open Secrets is one. If a donor has given to one candidate, he might give to another of similar orientation. It is superficial, but political giving can be rather superficial. Make a bigger gift and you can have a picture with the candidate. Make a larger gift you can be a host for a reception and be listed on the invitation. But even if the solicitor is working for a non-profit, this type of information may be useful if only to avoid making a mistake. Many donors will give to candidates of both major parties. That tells you something too.

Has the donor given to your cause?
If a donor has given to your organization before, then likely they will again. How long has the donor been supportive? At what levels? Is the support increasing or decreasing? Has it stopped and then started? Why? Perhaps whatever caused the break has changed. It might be that the donor has had a change in fortune, or it could be the organization has done something the donor does not like. If it the latter, has the organization done something to correct the perceived problem? It is good to know why there was a stoppage. Sometimes if a person has given a fixed amount repeatedly over many years, it is an indicator that they may like to add the cause in their estate plans. This would be an appropriate conversation to have because of the donor's abiding commitment to the cause. To approach a donor for a gift in ignorance of this information is a huge mistake.

When is the prospect's birthday or wedding anniversary?
Personally, I never like to send birthday cards to donors. It always struck me as a bit hokey. It may seem an obvious ploy to say to the donor that we are close and just like family. This is especially the case if there is no handwritten message on the card. A birthday card with no

personal message is so impersonal about what is a very personal matter. Some donors get a little uneasy if the advancement officer knows this information. Some people don't like to be reminded that they are another year older! Then too, our good friends at Facebook, remind us of our Facebook friends and family who have birthdays. Some Facebook people have thousands of "friends." Really?

I would never send a wedding anniversary card to a couple. It is just too much. Also, forgive me, sometimes the marriage is not going well. Even worse.

I do send Christmas/Happy New Year cards. I only do it if I hand write a personal message. No personal message; no card. As I sometimes point out to my Christian friends, Jesus only had 12 disciples. On the other hand, CEOs often send out cards to several thousand people. Even there, I would suggest that some on that list deserve a personal note. If your card is very Christian, it may not fly well with your prospects of different faiths. Season's Greetings and Happy New Year may be a better card, but it depends on the organization you represent and your relationship with the prospect.

Is the donor a friend with anyone on your Board or an important donor to your cause?
If a donor and a board member are friends, it sends all kinds of positive signals. Birds of a feather do, in fact, flock together. On the other hand, if a potential donor is a mortal enemy (Well, that's a bit strong.), of a board member, it is good to know that too. It is worth noting in the notes section of a person's record. On the other hand, situations change, and perhaps these two may have overcome past difficulties. A donor's friendship with a board member, or a significant donor to the effort, is important.

Does the prospect rely on a Certified Financial Planner (CFP), Attorney, or Accountant in matters related to gift giving or estate planning?
If these professionals are reputable, they will want to assure them-

selves that the cause is legitimate and the donor is making a prudent decision. In fact, often these professionals do not want to get into an argument with their client about their charitable cause. They would rather just agree and do what the client wants.

It is also true, that an advancement officer would do well to befriend these professional advisors if the opportunity presents itself. Oftentimes such advisors will suggest to a client that it would be prudent if the client had some charitable deductions to offset a capital gain in a given year. The professional advisor might suggest your cause. Buy that person a lunch for the referral! Reciprocate the courtesy if there is a donor looking for an advisor, and you believe the advisor to be sound. In fact, larger non-profits will have yearly or quarterly programs and lunches for these folks just for the reason of referrals. These programs are also helpful for solicitors to keep current with ever changing tax laws and regulations.

How does the prospect feel about endowment gifts?

I covered this topic in some detail in Chapter III, but when talking to the donor and looking for a large gift, this attitude becomes paramount. Some donors believe they can out-perform the investment officer at the non-profit. Why should donors make a gift now if they believe they can out-perform the charity's endowment manager? It is a consideration. On the other hand, it overlooks the good that can result from the gift right now, as well as into the future. It is the donor's decision, and they have made many good decisions so far. It's possible, if the donor is not explaining what they have in mind for the gift, the donor might just be trying politely to put it off. Also, if donors worry the organization may go bad, remind them children can go bad; foundations can go bad; their company could be sold; and government spends money inefficiently and ineffectively. I always smile when pointing out there is no perpetual guarantee of virtue in this life. Nonetheless, donors can leave a legacy for a noble cause that they seek to encourage.

How does the prospect feel about the death tax?

This becomes an important consideration with wealthy donors who are contemplating their estate plans. Wealth that is not distributed by the donor may be confiscated by the federal and state government at a certain percentage. As I said earlier, there is always talk about changing the death tax one way or the other.

Would the prospect have an interest in making a multi-year commitment rather than a lump sum gift?

If a non-profit has a large fundraising goal, and is seeking a large gift, it may seem to some donors that the gift amount is simply way more than they could prudently afford to make. Often a multi-year commitment is the way to go. It makes the overall gift bite size. It also gives the donor some leverage over the non-profit. If the non-profit goes in a direction with which donors profoundly disagrees, they can simply withhold the rest of the payments. Most importantly, it allows the donor to prudently manage the gift giving in a way that does not squeeze his other obligations.

Is there some program of your organization that would especially appeal to a donor?

The leadership of the non-profit likes gifts that have no restrictions or designations. It gives them great discretion. They can take advantage of opportunities that can't be seen in the immediate future. Perhaps there is opportunity to hire someone or to launch a new vital program that was not foreseen. On the other hand, the better a gift officer knows the donor and the better he knows his own organization and its needs, he may be able to suggest successfully a larger gift for something about which the donor would have real passion.

Once I met a lady who wanted to help a university in psychological counseling services for students. There were things in her life that prompted this concern. She asked many questions, and I quickly got her in front of the Director of Counseling. Now, the Director of

Counseling was thrilled that someone was interested in this vital part of the university. Counseling doesn't get much emphasis in the brochures and materials that students see. The donor wanted that there be notice given to students so they might know of the resources to help those who may be having some difficulties. This donor was especially thrilled to help. I have no doubt that the gifts she will give over time will be far greater because she is helping in a place that means more to her. I have seen this same thing in many of the non-profits for which I have worked.

What are the gift giving levels for various programs in your organization?

It is always good to have a menu that lays out the program areas and the donation levels along with how that donation will result in delivering a particular program service.

What types of recognitions would the organization give to the donor at the various gift levels?

Many people like to be recognized for their generosity whether at an event, in an annual report, or on the back of a program. If it in a printed program, the donors are listed by the level of the gift rather than a specific amount. The CEO may thank the donor from the podium at an event. Not only may it please the donor, such activities may encourage others in the future to do something similar. It is a way to thank the donor. The non-profit needs to think about the best way to thank its supporters. A personal thank you letter from the advancement officer is the minimum. If the gift is large, the program director, or the President should also send a personal thank you letter. Thank you letters from key leadership are always a good thing. Naming opportunities for large gifts for scholarships, rooms, buildings, awards, and programs are ways to recognize more permanently a donor's strategic support.

Might the donor prefer to remain anonymous?

A good number of donors prefer to keep their gifts anonymous and that should be respected. It is good to know what level of anonymity is preferred. For some it simply means they do not want to be listed in a printed program or a press release. Perhaps the reason is they do not want to be asked for a gift from another organization at the same level. Maybe they wish to keep it from friends for any number of reasons. I have had some donors who want an even greater level of anonymity. They did not want the gift referred to in internal documents with them as the source. Non-profits have no obligation to disclose to the public who is supporting them. Such recognitions can encourage others to ask them for support, but the donor's wish should be respected. If the donor wants a receipt, then it must be quite specific about the donor and the amount if they wish to claim a charitable deduction for tax purposes. It can be confusing as there are reasons within the organization to report donations from donors on internal records so people know what is going on. The way to do that sometimes is simply to list the gift associated with "anonymous." The main thing is to avoid having a person ask for a gift from a donor who has already given. Well, at least the donor would know in that case that the organization is protecting his anonymity.

Would the donor like to have a lunch or conversation with the Chief Executive Officer of the cause?

People who give at the largest levels may expect to visit with the CEO. They want to know that the CEO is going to follow through with the appropriate use of the gift. Or it may be that the donor feels they have earned it. The more high-level donors the CEO can meet with the better. In fact, it may be the CEO who closes the gift at the end of a process. The CEO is the chief witness for the case as to why a person should give. They also are the key person to execute the purpose of the gift. While it is good to have the CEO meet with the highest-level donors, the gift officer should not waste the CEO's time with what might be an average gift. The gift officer often must be part of setting up the CEO for the close of a major gift. In any large non-profit there are several high-level executives who might be useful in the cultivation process, and in following up. Some are good at it; some are not. The advancement officer should use his best judgment.

Might the donor have an interest to serve on an Advisory Board or Governing Board?

One effective tool in the box of the advancement officer is to offer an Advisory Board position to a donor. Advisory Boards are just that. They do not make decisions about the budget and they cannot hire or fire the CEO. There is no legal liability. Still these boards can be prestigious and usually there is an expectation of a minimal financial commitment each year. It also gives the advisory board member standing within the organization. Such a position could be a stepping stone toward membership on the governing Board.

Participation on the governing Board is for someone deeply committed to give treasure and time to the organization. This Board can hire or fire the CEO, and they approve or disapprove the budget. Their participation must be voted on by the current members. They also assume liabilities in case the organization violates the law or harms someone. They need to attend most of the quarterly meetings. Their service on a governing Board is for a set term. It is not to be offered lightly.

A FINAL NOTE

Having laid out these questions and their possible implications, sometimes a person will offer a gift without even being asked. For some of the largest gifts in which I have been involved, that has been the case. If the cause has been around a long time, and if it has touched the lives of many people, to some extent the advancement officer may just happen to be the person whom a donor approaches and asks how can they help. What does the organization need? Would you like a gift for such a program? That may lead to a large gift. The advancement officer gets the credit. Well done. Time spent with prospects is more productive than doing busy work at the desk.

ENDNOTES

1   *Acts* 20:35.

2   www.forbes.com; Bill Gates, April 2017; page 74.

3   www.forbes.com; Carlos Slim Helu, April 2017; page 74

4   Ritsuko Ando, "Japan's brokerages seize opportunities death set to rise," Reuters, August 28, 2014.

5   www.irs.gov/businesses/small-businesses-self-employed/estate-tax.

6   www.cei.org/blog/2017-unconstitutionality-index-18-federal-rules-every-law-congress-passes.

7   www.irs.com/articles/projected-us-tax-rates-2016.

8   Scott Greenberg, "Summary of the latest Federal Income Tax Data, 2015 Update," www.Taxfoundation.org, November 19, 2015.

9   Salman Masood, "Abdul Sattar Edhi, Pakistan's 'Father Teresa' Dies at 88," *The New York Times*, July 8, 2016.

10 www.aicpa.org.

11 "Giving USA: 2015 Was America's Most-Generous Year Ever," www.givingusa.org, June 13, 2016.

12 Patrick Henry, "And I Don't Care What It Is," page 41, *Journal of the American Academy of Religion*, March, 1981.

13 www.capenet.org, "Private School Facts."

14 "All 50 States and D.C. Charge Four Cancer Charities With Bilking Over $187 Million from Consumers," www.ftc, May 19, 2015.

15 www.fec.gov/law/law/shtml.

16 Sophia Bollag, "California ballot propositions rake in a record $473 million in campaign cash," *Los Angeles Times*, November 7, 2016.

17 *Ibid.*

18 www.ca-trusts.com.

19 "Federal Estate and Gift Tax Rates, Exemptions, and Exclusions, 1916-2014," www.taxfoundation.org.

20 "Does Your State Have an Estate or Inheritance Tax?" www.taxfoundation.org, May 5, 2015.

21 Ibid.

22 Kyle Pomerleau, "2016 Tax Brackets," www.taxfoundation.org, October 14, 2015.

23 Nicole Kaeding, "State Individual Income Tax Rates and Brackets for 2016," www.taxfoundation.org February 8, 2016.

24 www.foundationcenter.org.

25 James Piereson & Naomi Schaefer Riley, "Giving Back Isn't Only for Billionaires," *The Wall Street Journal*, December, 23, 2016.

26 Tamar Levin, "Princeton Settles Money Battle Over Gift," *The New York Times*, December 10, 2008.

27 *New York Daily News*, The Associated Press, April 30, 2016.

Acknowledgments

I have learned much in my career from many people, but I would like to thank especially Edwin J. Feulner, the late Ernest W. Lefever, Allan C. Carlson, Larry P. Arnn, Darla M. Romfo, the late Charles B. Runnels, and Andrew K. Benton.

My long-time friend and accomplished author, Bruce Herschensohn, gave me some excellent advice as I approached the project. My daughter Maureen designed the book and contributed thoughtful editorial comments, and my daughter Amy had some pithy but accurate insights. Responsibility for the final product is mine alone.

51492736R00108

Made in the USA
San Bernardino, CA
24 July 2017